Paperback
CRUSH

Paperback
CRUSH

THE TOTALLY RADICAL HISTORY
OF '80S AND '90S TEEN FICTION

by Gabrielle Moss

QUIRK BOOKS

PHILADELPHIA

TO JRB
who remains even better
than the real thing

Library of Congress Cataloging in Publication Number: 2017961245

ISBN: 978-1-68369-078-8

Printed in China
Typeset in Clarendon, Futura, and Sentinel

Designed by Andie Reid
Cover art by Ricky Mujica
Production management by John J. McGurk

Full publisher and artist credits appear on page 245. All illustrations
in this book are copyrighted by their respective copyright holders
(according to the original copyright or publication date) and
are reproduced for historical purposes. Any omission or incorrect
information should be transmitted to the author or publisher,
so it can be rectified in any future edition of this book.

Quirk Books
215 Church Street
Philadelphia, PA 19106
quirkbooks.com

10 9 8 7 6 5 4 3 2 1

Welcome to the Club!

Are you an adult with a full-time job who still dreams of switching places with your (nonexistent) identical twin? Are you a mature, sensible individual who cares about mature, sensible things like your 401(k) and gum health—but who also cares about those poor dopes who kept moving to Fear Street, even though it had a *well-documented* murder problem? Are you a loving, responsible parent who is only two cocktails away from shrieking, "Say hello to your friends, say hello to the peeeeeeople who care"?

If you answered yes to any of these questions: Welcome!

This book is a place of understanding. A place where you can sit down, get comfortable, and talk about Claudia Kishi's pumpkin earrings or that time Jessica Wakefield accidentally joined a cult while she was at the mall. Here you're among friends.

We're here to honor the young adult lit published after Judy Blume but before J. K. Rowling. These books often get a bad rap. People think of it as a time of superficial books about gossip, proms, and amnesia. But the YA novels that we hoarded from school book fairs taught us about female friendships, trusting ourselves, and speaking our minds—while also feeding us questionable lessons about what it means to be a woman and whose stories deserve to be told.

I know the nostalgic power of '80s and '90s young-adult lit firsthand. In the spring of 2016, I was in a major rut and decided there was only one way out: buying a crate of Sweet Valley High books on eBay. For the semi-reasonable price of $50, I could lose myself in the neon-tinted pop culture of my youth, with all its pointless catfights and ice-blue prom dresses.

I may have learned to read from educator-approved picture books about poky puppies and purple crayons, but I learned to become a *reader* from Sweet Valley High. In 1989, I begged my parents to buy me #32, *The New Jessica*, because I thought the girls on the cover had pretty hair. Little did I know that I'd be injecting the adventures of those pretty-haired Wakefield twins directly into my veins for the next four years.

Before Sweet Valley, I'd been a shy, unpopular dork. But after Sweet Valley, I was something much, much better: a shy, unpopular dork who could retreat into a pastel parallel universe.

There, everyone had friends, everyone was pretty, and everyone was special. My peers were stuck engaging with reality like *morons*, but with a trip to the library, I could become a California beauty queen, or an angsty teen living on a haunted street, or a clever babysitter loved by kids and adults alike.

I stopped reading tween lit in 1994, when I started middle school and became less interested in being elected prom queen and more interested in the prospect of burning down prom with my eerie telekinetic powers. But those books remained stuck in the back of my brain, and the slightest trigger—a geometric-print sweater, an attractive blonde teenager pitching a fit—brought back a rush of memories.

I knew they lingered there for some reason. But I didn't give myself permission to take a full-on journey into the past until that summer of existential dread. The books were a thirty-fourth birthday present to myself, and locking myself in my bedroom to devour a giant box of paperback novels from 1990 was a form of self-care that I thought would help me get my bearings. As I ripped through those books, I found more than nostalgia—though Jesus H. Wakefield, did I find nostalgia! I also found a record of my adolescent expectations—of the ideas about romance and womanhood and rebellion that had shaped me. I found the attitudes I'd end up embracing, and resisting, my entire life.

After that first box, I picked up more and more tween series until I had so many that I could no longer play off my behavior as a joke. I had contracted a compulsive need to buy books from the pre-Twilight era of teen literature, the days when no adult would be caught dead reading YA on the subway. I realized that I needed to share what I'd learned from rereading them and, more important, that I needed to justify spending so much money on Fear Street books instead of saving for a house.

That's the short version of how the book you are holding came to be. These are the stories that made us and, as I found out, the stories that can save us, even now. That alone makes them worth another look.

So now, if you'll excuse me, I have a Jungle Prom to ruin.

GIRL, YOU'LL BE A YOUNG ADULT SOON

So where did the young adult literature boom of the '80s and '90s come from? Well, the story starts at the dawn of YA—though experts don't agree on exactly when it dawned. Books from the original 1930s Nancy Drew stories to Laura Ingalls Wilder's 1932 book *Little House in the Big Woods* to the 1936 novel *Sue Barton, Student Nurse* by Helen Dore Boylston have all been held up as the first-ever YA novel. But a critical mass of people, including YA expert and former Young Adult Library Services Association president Michael Cart, say that it all started with Maureen Daly's *Seventeenth Summer*, a tale of summer lovin' published in 1942 that spoke directly to the hearts and wallets of postwar teen culture. *Seventeenth Summer* ushered in malt shop books, wholesome novels about teen girls who lived, loved, and never went past first base in an idealized America. Not long after, in 1944, New York Public Library librarian Margaret Scoggins changed the name of her *Library Journal* column on teen lit to "Books for Young Adults." In 1957, the Young Adult Library Services Division of the American Library Association was founded. And in 1966, the American Library Association changed the name of its list of books for a teenage reader to "Best Books for Young Adults." YA as we know it had been officially christened.

The '60s saw YA get serious. In 1967,

S. E. Hinton's *The Outsiders*, a novel about young gangsters in Oklahoma who are into emotional introspection and stabbing each other, set off what some have called the "first golden age of YA." Post-*Outsiders* YA channeled more of the zeitgeist of late '60s and '70s America, with authors like Judy Blume and Paul Zindel dramatizing previously forbidden topics like sexuality, drug use, and divorce.

But it wasn't until 1985 that a YA series landed on the *New York Times* best-seller list for the first time, thanks to Jessica and Elizabeth Wakefield, those foxy blonde sociopaths first introduced by Francine Pascal in 1983 (see page 104). They represented this new wave of YA, one that skipped narratives about teen trauma in favor of innocent romances that harkened back to the malt shop days, when girls were virgins, families were nuclear, and really bad stuff only happened to other people. These chaste romances created a brand-new revenue stream for publishers by getting the cash directly from the source: new marketing efforts allowed teens to bypass school or the library in favor of the mall bookstore.

Innovations in both sales technique and subject matter spread beyond teen romance, expanding, refreshing, and remarketing the YA worlds of suspense, drama, light comedy, and horror. Series like Baby-Sitters Club (page 141) or Saddle Club (page 73) were aimed at an audience a bit too young to envy the Wakefield sisters their Fiat, and legacy series like Nancy Drew and the Boxcar Children marched on with '80s and '90s makeovers. "Good" books for younger readers—the kind that teachers believed had literary value—were still being published, but this period was the first time the market was flooded with quickly churned-out paperbacks for young women, with plots that felt more like sitcoms or soap operas than earnest after-school specials. These books generally stepped away from the socially aware vibe of '70s YA, presenting stories of white, straight, thin, middle-to-upper-class heroines with few real problems. And like the '50s teen novels they harkened back to, these books posited that following society's rules was the path to popularity and joy.

The book packages also looked different from those that came before and after. Though '70s YA covers often featured subdued colors, '80s and '90s YA utilized perky pastels and neons. And though post–Harry Potter YA was dominated by trilogies and thick, sleekly designed hardcovers, '80s and '90s YA publishers specialized in paperback series with roughly one billion flimsy volumes, following the heroines' every move. Some YA series, like Gossip Girl, do carry the Wakefield torch—but they're rare.

Yet no matter how fluffy, overmarketed, heteronormative, and vapid the books of the '80s and '90s may have been, they did more than fuel the key transition from the realist YA fiction of the '70s to the sparkly YA fiction of the 2000s. (Though, I have to say, if you think Twilight invented sexy teen vampires, buckle up.). They helped turn us readers into the women we are today. Not because we embraced all the values the books implicitly endorsed, but because they gave us space to explore our identities, dream of the future, and, when the time came, engage in growth and rebellion by turning our backs on them. They validated girls' stories by putting them to paper—simple as that.

Does that make up for the fact that a lot of these books centered the stories of white rich thin heterosexual women with naturally straight hair? Of course not. These books were a mixed blessing, and for readers who didn't fit into the prescribed mold of the heroines, they were as alienating as they could be empowering. But their impact, and the way they shaped us into the protagonists of our own lives, is undeniable. They taught us that girls and girls' experiences mattered, that things our parents or teachers thought were frivolous were in fact important enough to spend a book or ten teasing the meaning out of. They taught us that we should say hello to our friends, because there's nothing better than them. They taught us that there was light at the end of most tunnels, and, if nothing else worked out, you could start over in California.

All those hours spent signing up for library wait lists, or scouring the shelves at Waldenbooks, or reading when you were supposed to be learning long division, really did matter. These are the books that taught us, implicitly, that reading could be fun—hell, that it should be fun! And the good lessons we learned from them are (mostly) worth remembering.

So come on in, friend. We've got a Scholastic Book Fair circular with all the best ones circled just for you.

AUTHOR'S NOTE:

We selected the books in this volume based on research, memory, and sometimes what we were able to hunt down. I'm sure we left out some favorites, and I swear we didn't do it on purpose—there are just so. many. series.

We also chose to include both young adult and middle grade novels—even though they are considered separate categories—because most tweens just read whatever looks good without consulting with the nearest publishing executive. Though I try to describe books, genres, and publishing trends correctly, it's far from an exact science (so please don't annihilate me on Twitter).

LYLAS, *Gabrielle*

A Selected Timeline of YA History

1930 *The Secret of the Old Clock*, the first Nancy Drew novel, is published.

1942 Maureen Daly's *Seventeenth Summer*, widely considered the first YA novel, is published.

1957 The American Library Association founds its Young Adult Library Services Division.

1967 S. E. Hinton's *The Outsiders* is published.

1970 Judy Blume's *Are You There, God? It's Me, Margaret* is published.

1971 Scholastic creates a school division to oversee its book clubs and magazines.

1979 The Choose Your Own Adventure series debuts.

1981 Scholastic enters the book fair business after acquiring California Book Fairs.

1982 The first "Banned Books Week" is founded by library activist Judith Krug.

1983 The Sweet Valley High series debuts with book #1, *Double Love*.

1985 Sweet Valley High becomes the first YA series to hit the *New York Times* Best-Seller List.

1986 *The Baby-Sitters Club #1: Kristy's Great Idea* is published.

1988 The Saddle Club series debuts.

1992 R. L. Stein's *Goosebumps #1: Welcome to Dead House* is published.

1997 J. K. Rowling's *Harry Potter and the Philosopher's Stone* is published in the UK.

1998 Rowling's debut, with the title *Harry Potter and the Sorcerer's Stone*, is published in the US.

2000 *New York Times* debuts its children's best-seller list.

2000 The American Library Association awards the inaugural Michael L. Printz Award for Excellence in Young Adult Literature to Walter Dean Myers's *Monster*.

2002 Cecily von Ziegesar's *Gossip Girl* is published.

2005 Stephenie Meyer's *Twilight* is published.

2012 *Publishers Weekly* reports that more than 55 percent of YA readers are older than 18.

CHAPTER 1

Love

FIRST KISSES,

FIRST BASE,

and

GOIN' ALL THE WAY

COUPLES

13

CHANGING PARTNERS

by M.E. Cooper

Scholastic 0-590-40235-8 / $2.50 US / $2.95 CAN

W here there are teens, there are love stories. Teenagers and romantic love go together like a drunk person and a six-day-old slice of pizza: it's a pairing destined to lead only to pain, but *you* try to keep them apart. Our teen years are when many of us have our first experiences with love (or with horndoggery masquerading as love), a fact that pop culture has reflected since at least the sixteenth century, when noted teenage goofballs Romeo and Juliet made some extremely questionable dating choices.

But love stories didn't become a huge part of YA publishing just because *l-u-v* is in teen culture's DNA. Romantic stories have been an integral part of every era of English-language publishing, from Samuel Richardson's 1740 book *Pamela, or Virtue Rewarded*, to the paperback "dime" novels of pre–Civil War America, such as *The Lost Heiress* by the phenomenally named Mrs. E. D. E. N. Southworth (yes, her real name was Emma Dorothy Eliza Nevitte Southworth! She was just *that* lucky!) to the 1940s pulp-fiction boom. Throughout it all, romance novels provided consistent work for female writers in eras when many other professional doors were closed to them. Much like the "throbbing members" chronicled in many a tale of ardor, you just can't keep romance novels down.

And up they came in the '80s, when "after years of being deluged with young adult books dealing with the unhappy realities of life, such as divorce, pregnancy outside of marriage, alcoholism, mental illness, and . . . child abuse, teenagers seem to want to read about something closer to their daily lives," as the promotional copy for the Wildfire series put it.

In fact, few young readers had "daily lives" like those of these fictional rich white teens from suburban California scrambling to find dates to the homecoming dance, but verisimilitude wasn't the point. Teens flocked to these books for a taste of glamorous high school life. Meanwhile parents wailed that YA romances were sexist and vapid and might encourage teens to engage in dry humping (some outraged 'rents even got a Wildfire promotional magazine pulled from shelves in 1981).

We'd expect old romance novels to be full of outdated cultural ideas, and the vast majority '80s and '90s teen romances are— few meet modern standards of healthy relationships, diversity, sex positivity, or proper shoulder-pad deployment. Yet many others are more progressive than you might expect, with more realism, egalitarian relationships, and empowered heroines than those pastel covers imply. Yet no matter where they fall on that continuum, these books were *beloved* by teens. As an academic paper presented at the 1984 annual meeting of the International Reading Association soothingly noted, "teachers may safely and enjoyably put a little romance into their reading programs." Let us, then, safely—maybe even enjoyably—swoon into the world of YA love stories.

A Series of Extremely Romantic Events: The YA Romance Series That Started It All

If you picked up a Wildfire book today, it wouldn't immediately stand out among other '80s romance novels. Their titles and tag lines aren't intriguing, and their cover models often sport awkward facial expressions that suggest they've just been told that their photo is going to be used in an ad for super-absorbent maxi pads. But this wasn't because Wildfire didn't know how to stand out in its field; rather, Wildfire was creating the field as the first teen romance series of the decade.

Series romance—so called because each book was branded similarly so that readers knew what to expect—had been around for grown-ups for ages, and by the mid-1970s, Harlequin was printing up to 150 million titles a year in the wish-fulfillment genre. They had existed on a smaller scale for teens in the '40s and '50s in malt shop books like Janet Lambert's Penny Parrish novels and Anne Emory's *Dinny Gordon*. But it wasn't until the beginning of the '80s that publishers began marketing series romances directly to the braces-and-acne crowd. After noticing that romance selections for their teen book club, like 1978's *Sixteen*

TK4286

Sixteen Can Be Sweet
by Maud Johnson

Can Be Sweet, always sold well, Scholastic created Wildfire in the hopes of capturing a similarly broad, if much younger, audience.

Wildfire was different from other standalone romances precisely because it traded on consistency. Although each volume was a self-contained story with its own cast of characters, it delivered certain similarities: an "average" teenaged girl dealing with a minor problem, like trouble with a teacher or lack of confidence; an appealing boy; no sex; no controversial content; and a happy ending. Even the covers looked similar to be easily spotted on a bookshelf or from across a store. Wildfire's advertising touted this sameness with slogans like "Every Young Girl's Dream of Love" and suggestions that if you liked one Wildfire book, "you'll love all the other Wildfire girls. They're a little bit of you!"

While "grown-up" romances of the late '70s and early '80s mostly had illustrated covers, YA romances of this era favored photos (and, apparently, turtlenecks), with couples who bravely stared down the reader instead of making bedroom eyes at each other.

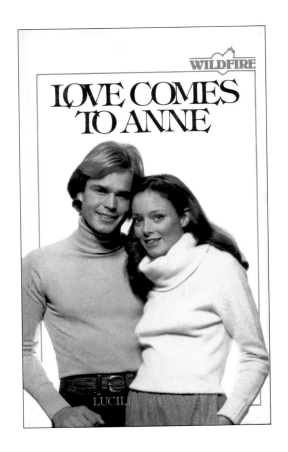

The branding worked: after Wildfire #1: *Love Comes to Anne* by Lucille S. Warner, was published in late 1979, the series caught on like, uh, wildfire. By 1982, Wildfire books had sold 2 million copies.

After witnessing Scholastic's unprecedented success with Wildfire, rival publisher Random House kicked off its own teen romance series, Sweet Dreams, in 1981. Sweet Dreams was also an immediate hit, with first print runs numbering 150,000 copies (to get a sense of how enormous that is, consider that *The Fault in Our Stars*, a 2012 novel by award-winning and then-already-successful author John Green, had a first print run of 150,000 copies). Where Wildfire cover girls often struck G-rated poses with male models, Sweet Dreams covers generally kept the sensuality threat level hovering somewhere between "cold fish" and "my dad makes me wear special chastity underpants" by depicting the heroine solo, with no boy in sight. Though none of these series' covers promised a *Wuthering Heights* for the Orange Julius generation, the models' habit of making eye contact with the reader helped convey that these were not your mother's romances. Typical romance cover models coyly averted their gazes, but these girls telegraphed that they were ready and willing to go after what they wanted.

With these two juggernauts leading the pack, a torrent of series about good girls in love followed: Sunfire, Wishing Star, Caprice, Windswept, Magic Moments, Two Hearts, Young Love, and First Love, among others. (Historians have yet to weigh in on why all '80s YA romance series names sound like brands of sensual massage oil.) Though some series

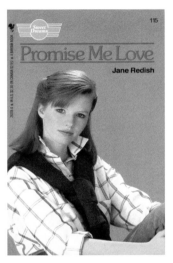

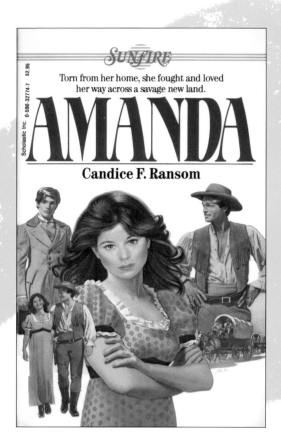

Sunfire was one of the few '80s romance series that used illustrations instead of photos, possibly because the covers featured not only the heroine (in a fancy dress to boot), but numerous other characters and other period-appropriate accessories (like a covered wagon) that would be simpler (and cheaper) to draw than to shoot.

put their unique spin on the format—Windswept had a mystery element and occasional ghosts, magic, and other supernatural threats, Wishing Star heroines dealt with personal problems like divorced parents or substance abuse, and Sunfire focused on a different girl in a different historical era in every volume, like a (slightly) sexier American Girl—they all aped Wildfire in pumping out stylistically similar but unconnected teen romances published with shocking frequency. Some series slapped new cover art on older books and published them as though they were brand-new, like Wishing Star's drinking drama *The Lost Summer*, which originally came out in 1977.

Some of these series only ran for a few volumes, but Wildfire bopped along until 1986, racking up an impressive 82 volumes. That number is dwarfed by the more than 250 titles Sweet Dreams put out before closing up shop in 1995, or the mind-boggling 236 titles First Love released between 1981 and 1987, before it was swept aside so that the market could be flooded with Sweet Valley High clones like Couples.

But while some folks might dismiss Wildfire as totally regressive and full of implications that teen girls should care only about dating, a closer look reveals something else. As scholar Carolyn Carpan wrote in *Sisters, Schoolgirls, and Sleuths: Girls' Series Books in America*, "rather than teaching girls to focus on love, marriage, and the baby carriage, many teen romance novels taught a generation of teenage girls that they could have it all—marriage, children, and careers." Sure, some Wildfires are pure '80s schmaltz (1982's *Sing about Us*, with a plot twist that hinges on a sexy belly-dancer costume!). Some have achingly punny taglines, like Jesse DuKore's *The Boy Barrier* ("Is tennis the only game she knows how to play?" Judging by how she's holding the racquet, I'm not confident she's even got that down.) But some Wildfires—like *Nice Girls Don't*, a 1984 volume by Caroline Cooney (who worked on dozens of series before writing *The Face on the Milk Carton*)—went so far as to turn

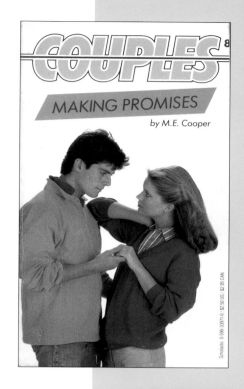

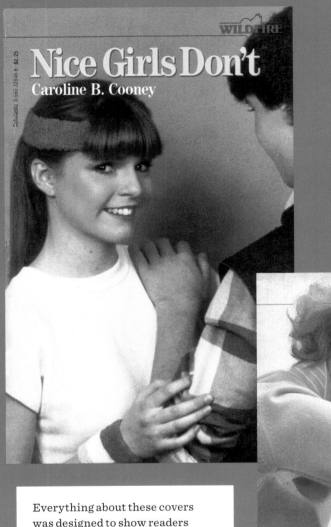

Nice Girls Don't
Caroline B. Cooney

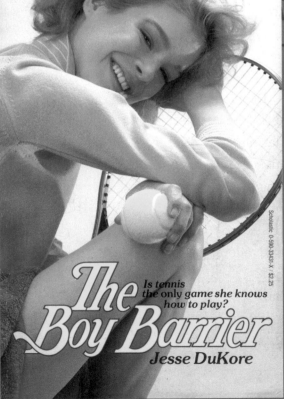

Is tennis the only game she knows how to play?

The Boy Barrier
Jesse DuKore

Everything about these covers was designed to show readers that these weren't their mothers' romance novels—from the extremely Pat Benatar headband to the models' poses (not to mention the nearly entirely cropped-out boy figure) that just barely hint at sexuality. Unlike '80s adult romances, which often did far more than hint at horniness, there's no lust-sodden gazes to be found here—just a thousand-yard stare at the reader.

feminist subtext into full-on text. *Nice Girls* follows Tory, a high school athlete fed up with both her school's sexism toward the girls' basketball team and society telling her she'd be a whole lot cuter if she didn't think so darn much. Tory isn't an innately confident and driven firebrand; she's confused, conflicted, and scared, as both the adults around her and her awful boyfriend Kenny suggest that she should give up on her quest for equality and take up a better hobby, like smiling vacantly. *Nice Girls* accurately captures the terror and exhilaration of standing up for what you believe in for the first time, and even Tory's romantic dilemma (hook up with progressive, supportive Jonathan, or stick with Kenny, who doesn't want women to drive *even though it is 1984*) reflects the deeply personal journey she's on.

66 **The stories took on some serious issues, but they were handled gently, and the emphasis was on clothes and boys and best friends. The difference? Girls had stronger roles in our books. My editor believed in strong female characters. They didn't wait for some boy to rescue them; they were able to stand on their own two feet.** 99

—CANDICE RANSOM, author of Thirteen, Sunfire, Windswept, and First Love titles, on '80s teen romance heroines

Despite being romances, a vast number of these books explore the pitfalls of relationships as much as the highlights, suggesting that dating for status is a soul-killing endeavor, that the popular jock you lust over might actually be a total buzzkill once you get to know him, and that romance is about respect and compatibility, not the buzz of smooching the captain of the football team. (For context, recall that even the 1985 film *The Breakfast Club*, which was far hipper and "edgier" than any of these books, suggested that women might be happier if they stopped being so weird and just wore a nice headband.) These weren't merely naive books that pretended that teen sexuality stopped at French-kissing; they were also fresh formulas infused with the lessons of second-wave feminism.

Writing for a YA Romance Series

How did all those Sweet Valleys, Wildfires, and other series arrive on Waldenbooks shelves week after week in the '80s and '90s? Did writers create their own plots, or was every twist planned by publishers? How did you even get a job writing them? What was it like to be part of a major YA literary phenomenon? To find out, I spoke to three accomplished authors who cut their teeth writing series YA: Candice Ransom (who worked on Sunfire, Boxcar Children, and more), Rhys Bowen (who wrote as Janet Quin-Harkin for Love Stories, Heartbreak Cafe, and more), and Caroline Cooney (who worked on Wildfire, Point Horror, and more).

RANSOM: I'd been trying to break into children's books since 1978 or so. Mind you, I knew I wanted to write for children since I was 15 and actually began that summer, writing a middle grade novel and submitting it to Harper and Row. By 1980 or 81, I'd tried "writing to trends," the result being a dismal YA-ish book about a boy who played Dungeons and Dragons. It was a disaster.

Then I found in *Writer's Digest* magazine a call for proposals by Ann Reit, editor at Scholastic, for [Wildfire]. I wrote three chapters and an outline for a romance book with little romance. Amazingly, Ann Reit called me on the phone. She didn't like that proposal, but she liked my writing. She asked if I'd consider writing a proposal for a new imprint of romantic suspense for teens called Windswept. This I could do. [That book,] *The Silvery Past* was published in 1982. From then on, I had a working relationship with Ann, who took me under her wing and taught me almost everything about writing and working with an editor.

I had so much fan mail that I devoted every Saturday to responding. Sometimes I'd get "class" letters, a letter from every student in a class, but the majority of my mail came from girls. . . . I also did many mall bookstore signings. Sometimes I'd have kids who'd already read my books waiting in line. And once, an intrepid bunch of girls found out where I lived and came to my house! It was great fun.

BOWEN: I had absolutely not considered writing YA before my agent asked me to. In fact, the whole YA genre hardly existed in 1980 when I wrote my first book. Mine was one of the books used to launch the Sweet Dreams line that suddenly made YA books popular. Before that, books for kids were bought by school libraries and adoring aunts. This was the first time that teens could buy their own books and dictate what they wanted to read. So I was right at the beginning, writing hugely popular books.

When I was asked to write "a teenage novel" I didn't think it was me. But I started writing, first person, and the voice just came to me. I was amazed how easy and fun it was.

Those early days of Sweet Dreams were very heady. We were celebrities. We got zillions of fan letters and if we went to a store, we were mobbed by teenage girls. Restrictions were that the books had to be wholesome. No graphic sex. But my heroines did have real-life problems: divorced parents, friends who were drinking too much. Essentially a slice of real life, but usually with a happy ending.

[The best part of writing series YA] was that I reached a huge number of readers, some of whom wrote to tell me they had never read a book before. The worst was snooty criticism from people who put them down as not being *Jane Eyre*. My comment was always that these readers would never have read *Jane Eyre*, and now they might because they had discovered that reading was fun. Another worst for me was the pressure to perform. My books were so much in demand that I couldn't write fast enough.

COONEY: Ann Reit, an editor at Scholastic, read a short story of mine in *Seventeen* magazine, and asked me to turn it into a paperback original teen romance. This was [Wildfire title] *An April Love Story*. . . . Later on, I began to write books for her by assignment. For example, she wanted to do a cheerleader series; she chose the names and circumstances of the girls and their friends, and I came up with the plots, about which we conferred and argued. I then wrote an outline, something that is difficult to do, because a book often takes on a shape of its own while you write. But in a series like this, you need to stick to the outline and that is terrific training.

I wrote books 1, 3, 5 and a few others [for Cheerleaders]. [The series] came out monthly, so several authors were involved. That meant your outline would affect the outline of the next book, which somebody else was writing. You also couldn't use a storyline another author had picked, so there were many conferences. I loved this. I think it is like architecture, where you design the best house you can, given the parameters of site, money, owner's needs. . . . There was complete freedom in the sense that it was my book, my dialogue, my morality, etc. But I would always thoroughly discuss the theme and plot with Ann first.

[Writing series books was] the best possible training. I've written over 90 books now and I credit my experience with series, a having to write fast and on demand and to order, as it were.

First Love Means Never Having to Say "Can I Copy Your Trig Notes?"

One of the greatest perks of adulthood (besides having the freedom to speak your mind, pursue your own interests, and eat five Stouffer's French bread pizzas in a single sitting) is never having to experience first love ever again. Sure, first love has its moments, and those pics of you and your prom date standing in your driveway remain totally adorable. But overall, first love tends to yield ten dramatic personal ultimatums delivered in a Wendy's parking lot for every one unforgettable evening spent looking at the stars. It's a bad deal.

But '80s YA books about first love put a gloss on things. In these fantasies of uncomplicated youth, trauma was minimized, hijinks were maximized, and everyone found someone to smooch. Sure, characters broke up (usually temporarily), fought (usually about nothing), and waded through obstacles, but all parties ended up happily partnered off by the end of the 150 pages. Though these books hit the same marks overall, they do so in different ways, and most of them end up falling into one of three major categories: Wacky First Love, Realistic First Love, and Soap Operatic First Love.

What qualifies as a Wacky First Love story? Well, how are ya doing on quirks? Does the heroine have some kooky thing she can't stop doing, like falling over her own feet? That's the case in Alida Young's 1986 book *Megan the Klutz,* in which the heroine is so absurdly clumsy that she cannot enjoy even a simple slice of pizza in front of her crush without getting cheese everywhere, tripping on a stray slice of soppressata, and, I assume, ending up trapped inside a meat locker.

Failing that, the heroine could have an adorable quirky problem, like Amy, the protagonist of R. L. Stine's 1989 master-work of teen romantic doofiness, *How I Broke Up with Ernie.* Amy wants to call it quits with Ernie. But due to a robust mix of her own indecision and Ernie being about as smart as a box of Nilla Wafers, it takes the whole damned book for her to pull it off, which leads to kooky scene after kooky scene of Ernie not realizing he's been dumped, even after Amy takes up with a new guy. (Maybe Ernie should try to date Megan the Klutz instead. She seems nice!)

But heroines who don't have a habit of being dumb or charmingly falling on their face into a pile of meat-garbage can still be wacky. They just need a scheme, like the ones found in Ellen Leroe's 1985 book *The Plot Against the Pom-Pom*

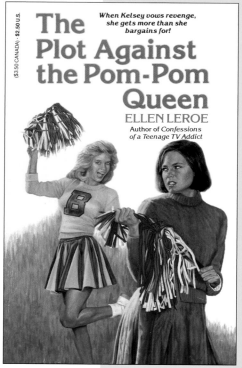

"Ellen Conford is funny again, sometimes wickedly so, in this collection of nine short stories."
—The New York Times Book Review

If This Is Love, I'll Take Spaghetti

Ellen Conford

Scholastic 0-590-32338-5 / $2.25 US / $2.95 CAN

A cover blurb from the *New York Times* was a rare occurrence for teen paperbacks in the days before Sweet Valley High broke onto the best-seller list (and way before the post–Harry Potter creation of a designated children's best-seller list), but Ellen Conford got a glowing write-up for this title (save for the lukewarm response to the collection's titular story). Whether or not an endorsement from the paper of record actually made a difference to discriminating young readers is hard to say.

Eve Bunting

Karen Kepplewhite Is the World's Best Kisser

Carol Newsom

Queen. Nerdy Kelsey crafts an elaborate plot to hook up with hottie Cal Lindsay, a jock who is "so sexy that girls under 17 would not be admitted to his classes without an accompanying parent." But rest assured, there is also a plot against the titular pom-pom queen, Taffy Foster, which involves getting Kelsey a makeover and utilizing something called a "Magical Male Grabber" (it's just a dating guide, get your mind out of the gutter). Wackiness abounds!

If you seek a book with a tamer scheme that still retains some wackiness, try Eve Bunting's 1983 novel *Karen Kepplewhite Is the World's Best Kisser*. The 13-year-old Karen plots to go from never-been-kissed to expert smoocher in the time before she throws a boy-girl party, which is to be attended by the extremely kissable Mark. Karen works towards her goal in a classic Wacky First Love fashion, practicing her make-out technique on inanimate objects and trying to understand the mysteries of romantic attraction in the run up to the big party, where everything turns out okay, as it always does.

At the opposite end of the spectrum are Realistic First Love stories, which dispense with schemes and quirks in favor of truthful emotional storytelling—and therefore don't always read as love stories at first blush. Ellen Conford's 1983 first-love-focused collection of short stories, *If This Is Love, I'll Take Spaghetti* takes on familiar scenarios like being let down by meeting your celebrity crush and a young girl's unhealthy fixation on her weight as the thing holding her back from true love, but because each story is only a few pages long, there's not much space for nuance.

But when Realistic First Love stories are executed powerfully, the end product is often a classic coming-of-age tale that just happens to include a romance. For instance, Marie Myung-Ok Lee's outstanding 1992 book *Finding My Voice*, which she published as Marie G. Lee, tells the story of high school senior Ellen's romance with classmate Tomper—against a backdrop of college admissions worries, her strict Korean immigrant parents, and the small-town

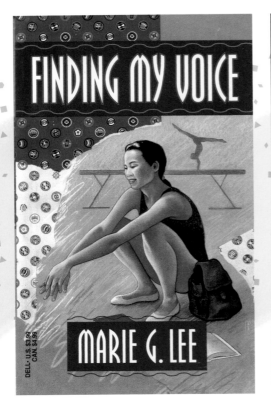

racists who assault and abuse her. But it's ultimately Ellen's relationship with Tomper that not only drives the plot but provides a skillful portrait of the intricacies of first love, while still addressing (and not sugar-coating) the realities faced by an Asian American teenager.

Lee's book wasn't the only one of the era to use a tender love story as a backdrop for groundbreaking work. Queer teen love stories had begun to emerge in the late '60s; John Donovan's *I'll Get There, It Better Be Worth the Trip*, published in 1969, is generally considered the first YA book to include queer romance, in the form of a same-sex kiss between the hero and his male friend. As you may recall, 1969 was the year of the Stonewall riots and thus not exactly a high point of tolerance, and so the book's editor, the storied Ursula Nordstrom of Harper & Row's Department of Books for Boys and

Girls, solicited prepublication blurbs from experts on childhood development and sexuality to confirm that, you know, gay teens exist. Still, even with the astonishingly progressive intent behind it, *I'll Get There* isn't exactly sunshine and rainbows: when the hero's beloved dog is killed, he concludes it was cosmic punishment for messing around with another guy. Other early same-sex romances, like Sandra Scoppettone's *Trying Hard to Hear You* from 1974 and *Happy Endings Are All Alike* from 1978, feature similar sadness. In *Trying Hard to Hear You,* one of the boys in the novel's gay couple dies in an accident, and in *Happy Endings*, although lesbian couple Jaret and Peggy are well-adjusted and their families work hard to understand and accept them, Jaret is nevertheless sexually assaulted by a bigot.

But one of the most celebrated LGBT romances came later, in 1982. *Annie on My Mind* by Nancy Garden was not, as many assume, the first YA romance between two girls—that honor is generally accorded to Rosa Guy's 1976 *Ruby*—but it was one of the first in which no violence or major sorrow befalls the queer lovebirds. Wealthy

Midcentury pulp novels about women lovers were notorious for unabashed and sensationalistic taglines, no doubt written with their male readership in mind. But here, the cover takes that traditional frankness and subverts it for a young, female reader: rather than play up the scandalous-slash-sinful nature of the relationship, it literally says "so what? There's nothing wrong."

"We love each other and so what? There's nothing wrong with that and we can't let anybody make something ugly out of it…."

HAPPY ENDINGS ARE ALL ALIKE

a novel by
Sandra Scoppettone

DELL • 93376 • 1.75

An ALA Best Book
For Young Adults

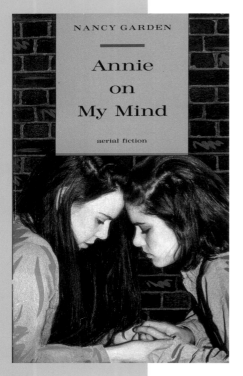

Liza and working-class Annie meet at the Metropolitan Museum of Art and fall hard for each other. And though their love is not without road bumps—homophobic school administrators attempt to have Liza kicked out (and succeed in getting two lesbian teachers fired), which leads Liza to temporarily dump Annie—the heart of the book isn't their trauma; it's the flush of first love captured in lines like, "The first day, I stood in the kitchen leaning against the counter watching Annie feed the cats, and I knew I wanted to do that forever." It was the first YA book to afford two girls in love the same sweet, rose-tinted realism granted to countless hetero couples (the *Kirkus* review of *Annie* opens with "Talk about meeting cute!" before going on to describe it as "a soupy romance"). In the end, Annie and Liza get that happily-ever-after that their predecessors were denied; the book's final words are "'Oh, god, I love you, too!'" Soupy, maybe, but also far more realistic in showing that not all queer love stories end in pain and heartbreak.

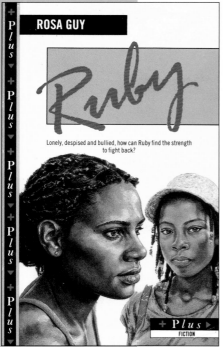

As *Annie* reprinted throughout the later '80s and early '90s, each new cover design gradually brought the girls closer and closer together, to the point of (gasp!) holding hands. Meanwhile, the earlier Ruby takes an angsty approach without even a whiff of romance.

Interestingly, for all the realism in these queer Realistic First Love stories, some of the covers opt for abstraction over specificity. The covers of *I'll Get There* and *Ruby* don't come close to suggesting a love story within, and while this is not necessarily a closeting, conscious choice, the artwork does afford the books enough invisibility to slip past conservative parents or librarians and into the hands of kids who needed them. With its "We love each other and so what?" cover line, *Happy Endings* took a bold step forward upon its publication in 1978, the year the LGBT pride flag was first flown. But just four years later, *Annie*, with its relatively unassuming cover, became a lightning rod for challenges and bans. (Granted, book banning became a much bigger phenomenon in the '80s than it had been in the past.) Garden's book was even burned in 1993 in Kansas by parents who wanted it removed from a school library, leading to an expensive, multiyear court case involving the ACLU that resulted in the book staying on shelves.

But maybe realistic love isn't your thing. Maybe you want a first love tale so absurd, so deranged, so full of pouty rich people and faked deaths that the librarian checking it out for you will roll her eyes. If this sounds like you, what you want is a Soap Operatic First Love story.

Many authors wrote soap operatic YA love stories in the '80s, but the soapiest had Francine Pascal's name stamped on the cover. The Caitlin series follows blazer-wearing rich girl Caitlin as she tries to negotiate her blazer-wearing first love while drunk on her own power (and surviving the nonstop plot twists that were synonymous with '80s Pascal).

The Caitlin books, which ran as a set of three trilogies (*Loving*, *Promises*, and *Forever*) published between 1985 and 1988, chart a decade or so in the life of the beautiful, terrible poor little rich girl as she repeatedly breaks up and makes up with her first love, Montana-based hunk Jed (Jed!), rides many horses, drives many luxury cars, is emotionally neglected by her family, accidentally

FRANCINE PASCAL

Caitlin

THE PROMISE TRILOGY: #2

PROMISES BROKEN

26156-8 ★ IN U.S. $2.95 (IN CANADA $3.50) ★ A BANTAM BOOK

lets an elementary schooler eat poison (it's okay, he survives, everyone calm down!), gets trapped in a mine, reconnects with her long-lost father, goes to college, is forced against her will to become a successful model, gets trapped in a barn fire, is forced against her will to become the head of a successful mining company, and is the subject of numerous unsuccessful plots by evil men who wish to "ruin" her.

Yes, these plots cover a lot more ground than mere first love. But at the end of the series, after all those implausibly wild rides, Caitlin has evolved from a wild, selfish monster to a boring and settled-down young woman in a long-term relationship. The only drama in the final volume comes courtesy of a surfing injury and a morally compromised race horse jockey. (*You used to be the terrible girl with evil destructive plans, Caitlin! You used to be fun. We're lucky we never had to see Jessica Wakefield laid so low.*)

Caitlin's "long black hair, her magnificent blue eyes and ivory complexion" were the first things readers learned about the character in an introductory letter from Francine Pascal at the end of *Sweet Valley High #18: Head Over Heels.*

FROM THE CREATOR OF SWEET VALLEY HIGH
FRANCINE PASCAL
Caitlin
THE LOVE TRILOGY: #3

$3.50 IN CANADA $3.95 / ★ A BANTAM BOOK

TRUE LOVE

Marie Myung-Ok Lee on her Journey to Publication

In 1992, *Finding My Voice* (page 30) became the first teen novel released by a major publisher with a contemporary Asian American protagonist by an Asian American author. Written by Marie Myung-Ok Lee as Marie G. Lee, the book won awards from the American Library Association and the International Reading Association, but publishing it was a struggle. "My agent was sending it out for over a year, I think," Lee told me. "A lot of [responses were], 'Oh, we just published somebody from Asia.'"

Lee started writing *Finding My Voice* without knowing much about children's publishing. "I wasn't 100 percent sure that it was a YA novel," she told me. "I thought it might be more of a *Catcher in the Rye* type of thing." But once she began submitting the book to editors, she found that the rejections focused not on genre but on race. "I think a lot of people found the very bald treatment of race in *Finding My Voice* to be off-putting," said Lee; the book deals frankly with heroine Ellen Sung's abuse by small-town racists, among other tough topics. "Nobody was really doing that then, so that made them uncomfortable . . . and that was why people passed on that book."

Publishers at the time had made superficial nods to diversity in YA (like including a single person of color in a series filled with white characters), but most books centered on young people of color were historical fiction, like Sook Nyul Choi's 1991 novel about the Japanese occupation of Korea, *Year of Impossible Goodbyes*. As a result, few novels released by major publishers focused on the experience of being a teen of color in contemporary America, not because no one was writing these stories, but rather due to publishing constrictions. "Ethnic literature [at the time] would just be the person being ethnic, as opposed to, the person could be ethnic and talking about what it's actually like being ethnic," Lee said.

Lee eventually found a home for the book, and "it was kind of in retrospect that people thought the book was groundbreaking." She also received criticism from individuals who thought that Ellen's strict parents were too stereotypical. Breaking ground means dealing with everyone's expectations: "I think when it's the first one," Lee said, "everyone wants to attack it, or it's never what you want."

Strange Love, or How I Learned to Stop Worrying and Love How Weird Everything Is

Most '80s and '90s YA romances were uninterested in taking risks with the formula; when you cracked open that aqua-and-hot-pink cover, you could count on a girl, a boy, and a series of small-yet-dramatic obstacles to their finding love. But a handful took a leap into weirdness, and got downright avant-garde as they did it.

The Choose Your Own Adventure series became an instant hit when it launched in 1979. Finally, the power to decide the circumstances of your own gruesome death was in your hands! The books' success revved up an army of knock-offs, from direct clones like the Twistaplot series to the Find Your Fate books, which allowed kids to create their own licensed merchandising adventure with Indiana Jones, Jem and the Holograms, or G. I. Joe (*To glamorize the military-industrial complex, turn to page 60!*). But the trend also led to a handful of books that kept the choose-your-fate framework while doing away with the adventure element entirely. Who needed to choose to dodge bloodthirsty reptiles who hungered for your tweenaged meats when you could . . . try to figure out mundane high school dating problems?

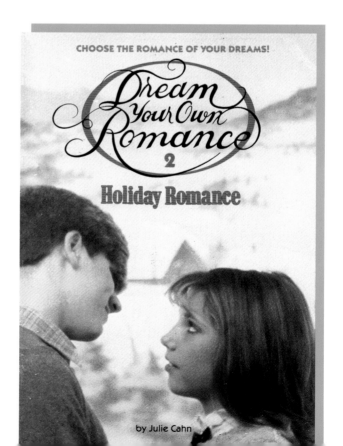

CHOOSE THE ROMANCE OF YOUR DREAMS!

Dream Your Own Romance
2
Holiday Romance

by Julie Cahn

Each Make Your Dreams Come True cover featured a photo of the heroine encased in a necklace chain, but unlike other YA covers with lockets (see pages 42–44), the jewelry wasn't there to symbolize anything, ahem, racy.

Step right into this story! Make all the big decisions—and see what happens....

Make Your Dreams Come True™

③

Worthy Opponents

If you were Jill, what would you do?

by **Nicole Carr**

0-446-32037-4 $2.25(U.S.A.) 0-446-32067-6 $2.50(CAN.)

Dream Your Own Romance (1983–4), Follow Your Heart Romances (1983–5), and the Make Your Dreams Come True series, which ran for only a single year in 1984, plopped you, the reader, down into the semirealistic lives of perky, heterosexual teen girls dealing with perky, heterosexual teen girl problems. For example, in Make Your Dreams Come True #3: *Worthy Opponents*, you're a popular high school junior named Jill (of course your name is Jill) who has to decide whether she wants to run for class president, manage the school hunk's campaign, attend a party alone, take vengeance on a school mean girl, and so on. To wit: "If you think Jill decides to go to the writers' conference, go to page 110. If you think Jill decides to stay home, go to page 121." Whoa, slow down there! You're trying to tell me I can experience the thrill of participating in school government *and* the wild, illicit high of deciding whether or not to attend a conference? All in one book? Understandably, this trend didn't last long—which is a shame. We never got to find out if Jill's secret admirer was a bloodthirsty reptile.

Another '80s trend to enjoy an awkward, brief romance with YA love stories was the body swap. Beginning in the '70s and continuing into the '80s, cinematic depictions of these comedic mix-ups were inexplicably popular, and filmmakers had tried swaps between mother and daughter (*Freaky Friday*), father and son (*Like Father, Like Son*; *Vice Versa*), grandfather and grandson (*18 Again!*), teenage boy and random old man (*Dream a Little Dream*), and Steve Martin and Lily Tomlin (*All of Me*). But until Susan Smith's novel *Changing Places*, no one had dared to do a body swap between a teenage girl and the boy she tongue-kisses.

Changing Places is a book that dares to ask the incredibly 1986 question, "What exactly are computers—like, are they magic boxes that can force you to switch bodies with your boyfriend?" For all-American teens Jenny Knudsen and Josh Friedman, the answer is a resounding yes! Due to the whims of some kind of cranky technological god, the pair of lovebirds have their bodies swapped while using a computer (trust me, it makes even less sense when you have all the details). Each is condemned to live as the other for a week, gaining knowledge of how the other half lives while also taking constant, scrupulous care to *never* look at the genitals on their new body, even

point

Some wishes shouldn't come true!

Changing Places

Susan Smith

Scholastic 0-590-33530-4 / $2.50 US / $3.95 CAN

When four teens get their wires crossed, they dial T-R-O-U-B-L-E!

PHONE CALLS

R.L. Stine

Author of How I Broke Up With Ernie

BC 65481/9 • $2.95 U.S. • $3.95 CAN • AN ARCHWAY PAPERBACK PUBLISHED BY POCKET BOOKS

Reach Out—and ZAP Someone!

The phone-frenzy starts when Diane calls her best friend Julie and convinces her to throw herself at super-jock Mick Wilson. Trouble is, Mick finds Julie about as intriguing as algebra! Julie is convinced the whole thing was Diane's idea of a joke. Well, two can play at the phone game. Julie calls Diane's brother Toby to plot a little sweet revenge. Before long, major phone warfare is declared, and Diane sets up the ultimate prank—a date to the Homecoming dance for Julie with exchange student Ramar, weirdo extraordinaire!

Now Julie desperately wants out of her date, Diane is starting to think Mick is pretty hot, and Toby secretly wants to go out with Julie. With all the laughter and confusion on the line, will they *ever* find the hotline to romance?

PRINTED IN U.S.A.

Unlike R. L. Stine's horror novels, *Phone Calls* features the title—not the author's name—in large type, positioning the concept as the main hook. Similarly, the "author of" tagline mentions his rom-com *How I Broke Up with Ernie* (see page 27) rather than the creepy-crawly backlist for which he's best known. For a similar pinked-up cover for a novel written by a horror author, check out Christopher Pike's entry in the Cheerleaders series (page 71).

though that's probably the first thing any of us would do in this situation. Since Jenny and Josh refuse to look at their new junk, they have time to focus on growing emotionally, and when they finally switch back, they understand that everyone has it hard, that a lot of their miscommunication was due to gender stereotyping—and that they are probably the only people on earth who would switch bodies with their partner and not fool around once. Maybe they *are* destined to be together!

But some literary experiments of this era were sui generis forays into a genre apparently created just for the hell of it, like 1990's bizarre R. L. Stine jam, *Phone Calls*. Before he became Stephen King for the retainer-wearing crowd (see chapter 7), Stine wrote teen romances, and he continued to write them well into his tenure as the unquestioned lord of mall-based terror; in fact, he was already six volumes into Fear Street when *Phone Calls* was published. What makes this book unusual? The entire narrative is, you guessed it, *phone calls* between friends, would-be lovers, and callous racist caricatures (the less said about Ramar, the exchange student and "weirdo extraordinaire," the better). Yet more perplexingly, the back cover copy implores us to "Reach Out—and ZAP someone!," whatever that means, and slanders poor Julie with the ultimate high-school neg, calling her "about as intriguing as algebra." (Better go to the school nurse for that burn, Julie!)

In theory, this is a unique, entertaining way to tell the very basic story of friends slash frenemies Julie and Diane, who get involved in an escalating war of prank phone calls and set each other up on a series of fake dates with boys at school. In practice, though, the book plays out as an avant-garde literary exercise pitched midway between Sleepover Friends and William Gaddis's *JR*. (Sample dialogue: "Hello?" "Hello, Mick? Do you know who this is?" "Huh?" "No? You'll have to guess." "What?") Reader beware! You're in for a book that innovates in a change-resistant field but doesn't break new ground in dramatizing the teenage psyche.

FICTION

P
POCKET
41012·1
$2.50

Forever...

A moving story of the end of innocence
by best-selling novelist

Judy Blume

The Last American Virgin

Before the Golden Age of YA, teens could learn about sex in precious few ways: progressive parents; an older sibling or friend; *The Canterbury Tales*; a pile of water-logged pornographic magazines found in the woods; or, most ill-advisedly, trial and error. But one place you definitely couldn't learn about sex was in early teen books (no one has written *Nancy Drew & the Mystery of Getting on Birth Control without My Dad Finding Out*, after all).

By the 1970s, novels like Judy Blume's *Deenie* (1973) and *Forever…* (1975) and Norma Fox Mazer's *Up in Seth's Room* (1979) had pushed back on the notion that teen sexuality was inherently a problem by featuring plotlines about topics like masturbation (gasp!) and nontraumatic consensual sex (double gasp!). But they weren't the only writers taking on teen bang-a-ramas. In 1978, Bruce and Carole Hart, writers for early seasons of *Sesame Street* and collaborators on Marlo Thomas's classic album *Free to Be…You and Me*, published *Sooner or Later*. The novel sported a cover that pioneered the trend of novels about teen sex that use a locket as a metaphor for … virginity (I guess?) and followed 13-year-old Jessie as she uses the magic of a mall makeover and positive thinking to convince hunky local 17-year-old musician Michael that she is a hot-to-trot 16-year-old (only to

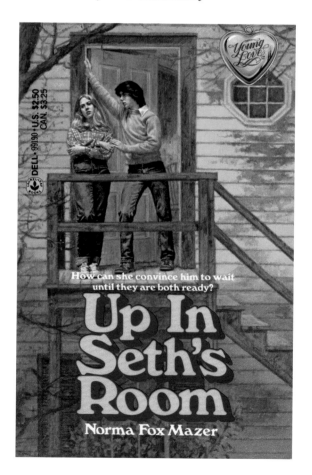

eventually reveal the truth, and scramble to salvage their relationship). The story became so popular that it was continued in two other books (and a TV movie in 1979), making it one of the few series to address sex that successfully made the leap between the '70s and '80s.

In 1981's follow-up, *Waiting Games*, Jessie and Michael decide they're still committed, despite their not-that-large-but-still-weird age gap and Michael's tendency to jump out of the car and yell "Whoa!" at the night sky every time Jessie says that they can't go all the way. Eventually, Jessie and Michael "do it," in a situation where the consent is hazy by today's standards, and the action lasts for about 45 seconds by any era's standards. Jessie worries about pregnancy, she and Michael drift apart, and they split up so he can follow his rock star dreams to California. Eventually, they reunite in 1991's *Now or Never*. *Waiting Games* tries to engage with the era's changing sexual standards—as Jessie exclaims,

AVON/55079 / $1.95

A NOVEL BY
BRUCE AND CAROLE HART

SOONER
OR LATER

BASED ON THEIR SCREENPLAY

NOW A MAJOR TELEVISION MOTION PICTURE

As evidenced by this cover (as well as the two covers on pages 42–43), there's just something about a locket that screams "virginity is about to be lost!" In the case of *Forever . . .*, the necklace is in fact a plot point, but regardless of the story, the symbolism fits to an almost ridiculously literal degree: something private finally opened up . . . okay, ew.

"I mean, there's this Sexual Revolution going on, and here I am a Conscientious Objector!"—but unlike the sex-positive heroines of '70s YA, Jessie isn't sure how she fits in with all these changing ideas about sexuality. She muses that sexually, she's "slow. For my age" and then compares herself negatively to "teen-aged girls who wound up at spring training camp with the Pittsburgh Steelers, or the ones who bumped into Mick Jagger on the plane to Akron." Furthermore, the action is almost entirely driven by Michael's desire, and Jessie seems to be interested in sex only to keep Michael happy. The book doesn't quite push back on that dynamic, which seems iffy to a modern reader, but is an interesting reflection of its time; if you just go by Judy Blume or Norma Klein, you might think that the average '80s high school girl was constantly owning her own sexuality and orgasming all over the damn place, but Jessie's confused, tentative first sexual experience was probably just as common, if not more so.

And speaking of Norma Klein, her 1981 novel *Domestic Arrangements* presents a similarly complicated image of teen female sexuality. The book follows 14-year-old Tatiana, the youngest daughter of an artsy New York City bohemian clan (think *The Royal Tenenbaums* except everyone is Jewish and likes each other). Tatiana is a

AVON/FLARE/79012/$2.50   FLARE ORIGINAL NOVEL

WAITING GAMES

BY BRUCE AND CAROLE HART

A SEQUEL TO THE NATIONAL BESTSELLER, **SOONER OR LATER**

Domestic Arrangements is one of several now-vintage YA novels reissued by Lizzie Skurnick Books, an imprint of Ig Publishing that republished and repackaged out-of-print children's and YA novels from the pre-1990s era. Besides a new cover to replace this original illustration, the reissue included a foreword from none other than Judy Blume.

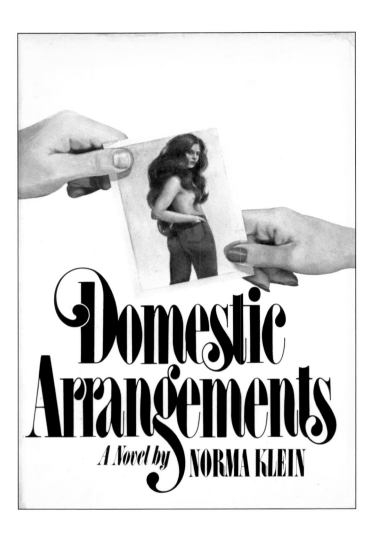

film actress gaining attention for a seminude scene she did in an art film (shades of Brooke Shields in *Pretty Baby* and *Blue Lagoon*) and also experimenting with gettin' it on. The sex Tatiana has with her boyfriend, although mildly explicit, isn't shocking or tawdry; it's respectful and all parties involved seem into it. Rather, the real meat of the book is about Tatiana's parents becoming estranged and taking their own lovers, while Tatiana, a bit brassier than the average suburbanite Blume heroine, wonders if her love with her boyfriend is real, or just based around, as she puts it, "fucking." And yet a *Kirkus* review called the novel "blah"! Perhaps, for the reviewer, it was; YA sex novels had oversaturated the market (to the point where sexually active 14-year-old who swears like a longshoreman and appears in her underpants on film is boring) and faded from popularity by the end of the decade.

But this wasn't just because teens had moved on to a new trend. The world itself was changing. In 1981, the same year *Waiting Games* and *Domestic Arrangements* were released, the first cases of AIDS and HIV in the U.S. were reported. Teen sex in YA may have already been on its way out, but the public health crisis certainly hastened its exit. Now, experimenting with sex wasn't just a rite of passage; it was a risky situation in which not knowing enough could get you killed (as we'll see in the rush of HIV and AIDS cautionary tales in the '90s; see page 199). The tagline on a later edition of *Domestic Arrangements* made that change in attitude crystal clear: "She learned about sex too soon—Now she has to learn about love."

CHAPTER 2

Friends

BFFS, FRENEMIES, *and* TWEENAGE SOCIAL CLUBS

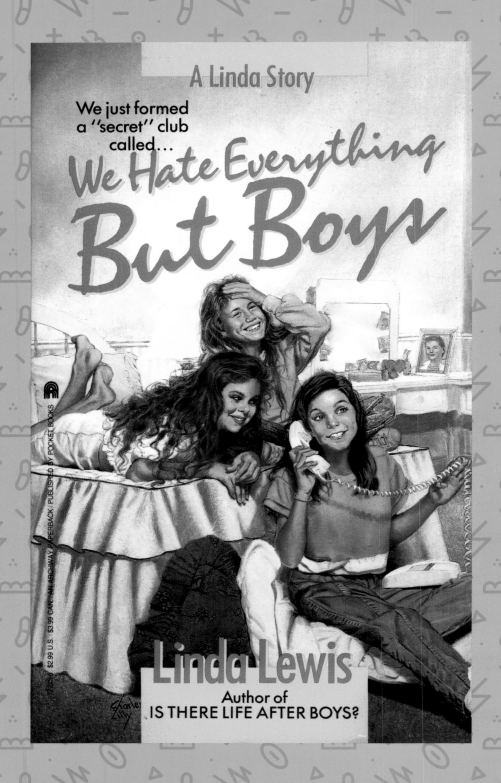

Novels about tween female friendships haven't just remained popular through the years because figuring out the nuances of social interaction is one of the only nonschool pursuits available to people too young to drive. It's because the basic format of the friendship novel—friends tackle a problem together, have a moment of doubt, but come out the other side victorious—can be easily adapted to any era. In fact, teen friendship novels have changed remarkably little since they were first introduced at the beginning of the twentieth century. And I don't mean that in the way a drama teacher would say, "well really, Shakespeare was the first rapper." They are eerily similar.

Take Gertrude W. Morrison's Girls of Central High series, published from 1914 to 1919. The book's group of pals includes the strong leader, the sporty friend, the wacky twins, the one from an arty family, and the rich one; once assembled, the friends play on school sports teams, annoy their uptight teachers, butt heads with the school bully, prank their classmates, raise money for a family in dire financial straits and, on one memorable occasion, set off firecrackers indoors (in 1919! The year many US women got the right to vote!). It's not that this series is wildly progressive and forward-looking—these are books in which characters sternly use the word "scamp" and discuss whether a codfish would make a good Christmas present. It's just that these plots and character types are timeless.

But for all their enduring themes and happy endings, friendship novels have their shortcomings. As society evolves, these books don't instantly catch up. Middle grade novels from the '80s rarely portrayed girls of color hanging out and doing normal tween stuff without a bunch of white girls also present, despite having been published years after the peak of the civil rights struggle. And all too often, these books glossed over the very real pain young female friends can cause one another. But though they're far from perfect, they considered female friendships worthy of topline billing—decades before most films, TV shows, or grown-up novels agreed.

Hittin' the Club

You know that Frank Sinatra song, "You're Nobody til Somebody Loves You"? Well, in the realm of '80s and early '90s girls' novels, you were nobody til somebody wanted to start a club with you. Sure, needlessly intricate tween social infrastructure dates back at least to the bust-obsessed Pre-Teen Sensations of Judy Blume's 1970 novel *Are You There, God? It's Me, Margaret,* but the mid-'80s popularity of the Baby-Sitters Club (see page 141) sent publishers scrambling for quick ways to cash in on tween crews. The result was a flood of books that implied that you couldn't put two 12-year-old girls alone in a room together without one appointing the other one treasurer.

But the tween club frenzy didn't appear overnight. In fact, one series in particular connected the '70s-era Pre-Teen Sensations with the club-crazy world that came after. Betsey Haynes's 1976 novel *The Against Taffy Sinclair Club* was exactly what it sounds like: a book about a group of fifth-grade girls who form a club specifically to rag on their classmate Taffy. What has Taffy done to become so loathed? It's not important (but for the record, it's that she grew boobs before they did). What is important is that the ATSC girls undertake all the '70s equivalents of Instagram

A BANTAM-SKYLARK BOOK

TAFFY WAS HARD TO TAKE
WHEN SHE WAS JUST PRETTY, BUT NOW...

THE AGAINST
TAFFY SINCLAIR CLUB
BY BETSY HAYNES

trolling: creating a slam book all about Taffy, spray painting "Taffy Sinclair Has Her Period" on the school sidewalk, and other mundane middle-school cruelties. The slam book falls into the wrong hands, and Taffy's mother freaks out on the ATSC. Eventually we learn that protagonist Jana is actually worked up over her deadbeat dad and taking it out on the poor Taffster: "I hated myself, and I kept thinking that it was no wonder that Taffy Sinclair hated me, too." Chastened, the girls vow to change their cruel ways, becoming a newer, kinder club called . . . the Fabulous Five!

At first blush, the titles in the Fabulous Five series, which comprised thirty-two volumes published between 1988 and 1992, look more like a Baby-Sitters Club knock-off than the tales of a rehabilitation group for reformed school bullies, but the books were indeed a deft(ish) import of familiar characters into a new, kinder era of friendship novels. Before the start of the spin-off series, the Fab

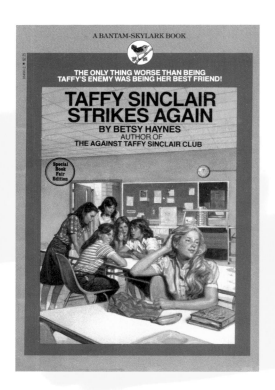

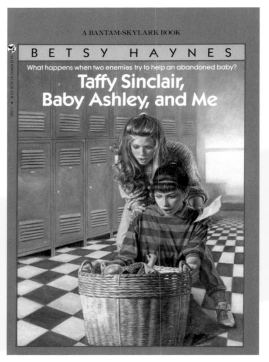

gang had a whole set of adventures, in the 1984 sequel *Taffy Sinclair Strikes Again* (plot twist: they still totally hate Taffy Sinclair) and the 1987 follow-up *Taffy Sinclair, Baby Ashley, and Me* (in which a member of the Fab Five and Taffy find an abandoned baby, which somehow *still* turns into a petty sixth-grade power struggle). But eventually Taffy leaves town and the gang transitions to dealing with lower-key issues like losing TV privileges (in *The Great TV Turnoff*) and running a taxi service (in *Teen Taxi*), rather than trying to emotionally destroy a fellow child. In that transition, they showed what changed in the Great Friendship Clubbening of the '80s: dramatic girl-on-girl hatred was out; kind, supportive tween friendships were in.

The Fabulous Five's convoluted origin story was certainly the exception, however; most groups had an origin story so simple, you could write it on a friendship bracelet. The club in Linda Lewis's

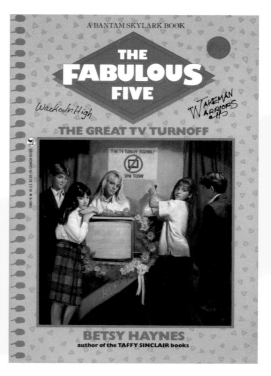

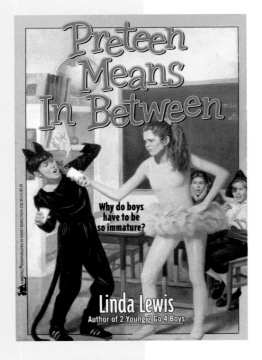

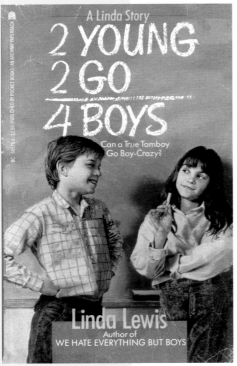

1985 novel *We Hate Everything but Boys* (see page 50), for instance, was committed to a dead-simple premise, which continued through all eleven volumes of the subsequent Linda series (named for the series star, who shares a name with the author, go figure), including the 1993's spin-off *Preteen Means In Between* and the 1988 prequel *2 Young 2 Go 4 Boys*: Linda and her friends are totally gaga for dudes. But their club isn't just about plotting to make contact with your crush; they branch out into other related issues, such as the importance of finding a "cry spot" in the park where you weep about your romantic difficulties (that's a dating skill you'll want to hold on to through your twenties, girls!).

Other club series managed to set up a straightforward premise and immediately poke holes in it. Deirdre Corey's Friends 4-Ever series, which debuted in 1990, chronicles a group of friends who become pen pals to keep up with their friend Molly after she moves away, which

Probably the only series "by Lindas, about Lindas," the Linda series ran for 11 books, following the characters from fourth grade all the way through senior year of high school.

2 SWEET 2 B 4-GOTTEN **#3**
Deirdre Corey

P.S. WE'LL MISS YOU **#1**
Deirdre Corey

checks out—each volume is titled after cutesy, letter-writing-related puns like *P.S. We'll Miss You* and *2 Sweet 2 B 4-Gotten* (and people blame cell phones for poor spelling!). Except, midway through the series, Molly moves back! But all the Friends 4-Ever keep writing each other letters! Even though they live in the same town and see each other all the time! Perhaps their true best friend was adhering to organizational protocol at all costs.

Unlike Linda and her boy-obsessed crew, or the correspondence-crazy Friends, the gang in Betsy Haynes's 1995–6 Boy Talk series (not to be confused with Girl Talk; see page 61) formed a club not to kvetch about their own dating difficulties but to micromanage the love lives of others. Best pals Su-Su, Joni, and Crystal are sick of sitting around and having names that make them sound like they work at a food co-op—they want to provide romantic advice to the public! With that premise, the girls proceeded to dish out dating guidance for nine books, despite having no qualifications besides

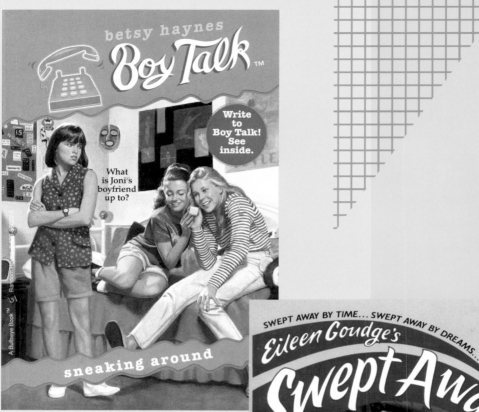

All entries in the Swept Away time-travel series had pun-tastic titles alluding to the time period of choice, but some of them—like *Gone with the Wish* (Civil War era) and *Spell Bound* (Salem circa the witch trials)—took their heroines to eras that were problematic at best and dangerous at worst. But romance was found nonetheless!

moxie, an undying desire to know everyone's personal business, and parents who didn't care how long they tied up the phone.

Tween fiction offered a club for almost everyone, including the aspiring time traveler. As has been well-established by the acclaimed 1989 documentary film *Back to the Future Part II*, mad professors rarely included female teens in their time travel experiments, preferring instead to knock them unconscious and leave them in an alley. It's like they'd never even heard of Title IX! Luckily, the girls of the Swept Away series worked tirelessly from 1986 to 1987 to close the time travel gender gap. Why time travel? Oh, for a bunch of reasons: to witness historical events, to authenticate family heirlooms, to prevent the teen versions of their moms from dating guys with unappealing names like Dick Flick, and so on. The science is a bit head-scratching—the girls transport themselves via a machine jury-rigged from the town library's modem and a purloined laser gun, which . . . sure?—and the friends have a downright laissez-faire attitude vis-à-vis potential repercussions. So you're warping the fabric of the universe? Big deal! Party with Elvis! Manipulate the teen version of your mom! Act like a total narc at Woodstock! Who cares? Time clearly has no value if you can manipulate it with some junk you got at the library! Still, the series did give teen girls credit for hacking time travel just like their male peers, which counts for something. Remember, a book can be culturally pioneering and also not very good at the same time.

On the complete opposite of the plausibility spectrum was Susan Saunders's ultra-realistic Sleepover Friends. The series ran for thirty-eight volumes from 1987 to 1991, a genuine eternity in tween fiction, all of it predicated on the simple fact that sleepovers are utterly bitchin'. Sure, the friends had individual personalities, or as individual as you get in these series: Kate the bossy one, Lauren the athlete, Patti the studious one, Stephanie the arty one who is also the one who used to live in the city. And some adventures took place during the day—#11, *Stephanie's Family Secret*, memorably

#3 Kate's Surprise
Susan Saunders

Scholastic 0-590-40643-4 / $2.50 US / $3.50 CAN

#2 Starring Stephanie
Susan Saunders

Scholastic 0-590-40642-6 / $2.50 US / $3.50 CAN

involved winning a burro in a contest. But the true glory of these books was in the sleepovers themselves, which were described in achingly luxurious detail: what junk foods the girls ate, how they wasted time, how no one's parents ever seemed to give them any guff about it ("We stayed up really late watching a double feature on Chiller Theater. . . . And we slept late the next morning. When we finally got up, Stephanie's parents had blueberry-banana pancakes waiting for us"). For those of us who were roused early on weekend mornings for chores or church, or just didn't have any friends to sit around eating blueberry-banana pancakes with, Sleepover Friends was the tween equivalent of reading about Gwyneth Paltrow's Paris apartment in *Architectural Digest*.

And yet all was not entirely normal in the Sleepover-verse. As YA blogs the *Dairi Burger* and *Sleepover Friends Forever* have astutely noted, the cover of #13: *Patti's Secret Wish* depicts the friends in a bookstore, surrounded by middle-grade series like the Baby-Sitters

APPLE PAPERBACKS

SLEEPOVER FRIENDS

What is Patti up to?

#13 Patti's Secret Wish
Susan Saunders

SCHOLASTIC   Scholastic 0-590-42301-0 / $2.50 US / $3.50 CAN

For young book geeks (and, okay, for us adult book geeks too) the mise-en-abyme of Sleepover Friends #13 is pretty much catnip; there's a Gymnasts title third from the left, and a Baby-Sitters Club book second from the right. (Whether any tween girls cared about a book called *Quarks* is hard to say.)

Club, the Gymnasts, and . . . *Sleepover Friends #11: Stephanie's Family Secret*! *How is this possible?* Are the Sleepover Friends celebrities within their own timeline? Was some kind of inception afoot here? Maybe your friends' parents let them bend the laws of reality, but in my house, you'll obey my rules, young lady!

Sadly, no other tween club series shredded the fabric of existence, but Girl Talk, a board game turned TV show turned book series, came close. The game, a gussied-up version of "truth or dare" that directed players to perform humiliating tasks like "have a conversation with a piece of furniture" and "drink a glass of water without using your hands," came out in 1988. Naturally, it was an enormous hit with tween girls. And you know what everyone does when they have a hit board game for girls on their hands: turn it into a TV show! Sadly, when the *Girl Talk* TV program debuted in 1989, it was not an emotional-torture version of *Double Dare* but a simple variety show with skits hosted by a 12-year-old Sarah Michelle

1

Can these girls survive seventh grade?

Golden® /0-307-22001

WELCOME TO JUNIOR HIGH!

By L. E. Blair

22001

Gellar that lasted only two episodes.

But in 1990, the Girl Talkiverse introduced a new concept: books! And these weren't popular just for a series based on a perversely cruel board game; they were tremendously popular, period, with forty-five volumes published in three years. (A number were ghost-written by K. A. Applegate, the YA and middle grade powerhouse behind the Animorphs series and Newbery Award–winning *The One and Only Ivan*.) The "talk" conceit came in the form of passages of transcribed phone calls, which shook up the conventional friendship book format a bit. Like R. L. Stine's similarly experimental dialogue-only romance (see page 41), they're something of a stylistic precursor to contemporary YA like Lauren Myracle's 2004 novel *ttyl* and its sequels. However, in the Girl Talk novels, the phone call sections usually take three pages to explain something that could have been dealt with in three lines of prose. Beyond these mild structural innovations, Girl Talk dutifully played by the club series rulebook. Sabrina, Allison, Katie, and Randy had standard middle school novel personalities—the chatty one, the political one, the anal-retentive one, and the one whose whole personality is that she is from New York City—and got into standard middle school misadventures, like trying to become models and running for class president.

And naturally, no discussion of clubs is complete without mentioning some of the oldest female clubs around: sororities. YA literature in the '80s was lousy with under-18 sororities, despite such societies being uncommon in the real world; in fact, fraternities and sororities have been banned in California public schools since the '60s, which would make Sweet Valley's Pi Beta Alpha illegal (not that we're surprised Jessica Wakefield is a criminal). The most notable example is Marjorie Sharmat's *Sorority Sisters*, which ran for eight volumes from 1986 to 1987. The series chronicles Palm Canyon High School's bloodless yet brutal battles between the snobs of Chi Kappa and the down-to-earth ladies of the Pack, a new

sorority formed by girls disgusted by Chi Kappa's pretentiousness (also, they tried to get into Chi Kappa and couldn't). The constant bickering invites the question: why not ditch the organizational infighting and just have, you know, friends? (Because then there'd be no series, duh.)

Finally, lest you write off all club book series as frivolous, there were in fact a handful that addressed topics more substantial than French-braiding. The NEATE series, put out by African American publisher Just Us Books between 1992 and 1994, had its mixed-gender group of members—that'd be Naimah, Elizabeth, Anthony, Tayesha, and Eddie, aka NEATE—join forces to deal with pressing social issues, like helping Naimah's mother win a

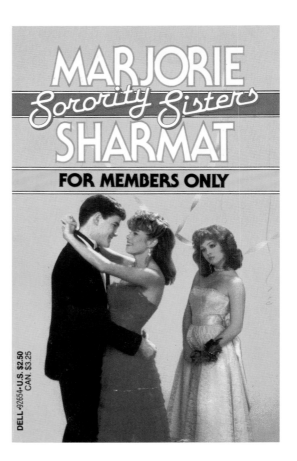

MARJORIE *Sorority Sisters* SHARMAT

FOR MEMBERS ONLY

DELL-92654-U.S. $2.50
CAN. $3.25

city council race against an unrepentant racist, raising awareness about gerrymandering, or saving a refugee shelter from closure. The magic of NEATE is that the books didn't save this stuff for a Very Special Edition; they mixed social concerns in with more traditional middle grade stories about talent shows and demanding parents. As one of the rare series in the era to focus exclusively on African American tweens, NEATE managed to thread the needle between "real world issues" and "kid-level relationship drama" without coming off preachy—or worse, boring—showing how easily your average tween series could have packed more meaning and substance in with their tales of pizza parties and sleepovers, if they'd only tried.

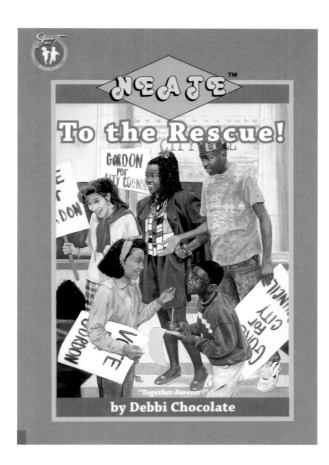

In a review, *Publishers Weekly* praised *NEATE: To the Rescue!* as "a cut above the typical mass-market YA offering," but found its "contemplative tone" and subject material "a bit at odds with the sprightly cover artwork."

The Story of Just Us Books

In the late 1980s, Wade Hudson and his wife, Cheryl Willis Hudson, couldn't find the kinds of children's books they wanted their two children to read. While the children's publishing business was exploding, the Hudsons saw one very obvious gap: "there were very few Black authors and illustrators creating books for children and young adults," as Wade told me.

Though African American authors like Walter Dean Myers, Mildred D. Taylor, Virginia Hamilton, and Patricia McKissack had been publishing books that "[drew] from Black experiences and [created] Black characters," major publishers were still more interested in publishing biographies of the same handful of famous African Americans (Dr. Martin Luther King Jr., Harriet Tubman) than they were in stories of contemporary African American life. "Many white editors didn't really understand Black life, Black culture, etc.," said Wade. The Hudsons had firsthand experience with this kind of thinking—as they recount on their website, while trying to publish a children's book they had created together called *AFRO-BETS ABC Book*, they were told by one editor, "There's no market for Black children's books."

"I don't know how many times I have heard over the years Black writers say they were told by white editors that a manuscript they had submitted didn't seem plausible," Wade said. "Obviously, Black life was foreign to many of these white editors."

Ultimately the Hudsons published *AFRO-BETS* themselves in 1987, and in 1988, they founded one of the first publishing companies dedicated to African American children's books: Just Us Books. Though the couple had no prior experience running a company, they believed in their vision and put their life savings toward building the business.

It paid off. Thirty years into its existence, the Hudsons still run Just Us, which has published dozens upon dozens of young adult and children's titles (including the NEATE series, page 64), some of which have gone on to become best sellers and win awards like the prestigious Coretta Scott King Illustration Honor from the American Library Association. Wade and Cheryl have each written and published over twenty books, both with Just Us and with other publishers, and in 2004, Just Us launched its first imprint, Sankofa Books, to bring out-of-print classic books about African Americans back to the market. Through the years, the Hudsons have seen the publishing industry at large become more interested and invested in diversity. "It has been a gradual change prompted by agitation and prodding by people of color," said Wade, "and by those who support diversity in children's and young adult literature." But, he notes, "Book publishing, like other industries, is often driven by trends and not by a commitment to a cause or to do what is right and just."

"Books written by people of color have proven themselves in the marketplace," Wade said, mentioning best-selling and award-winning novels by Jason Reynolds, Jacqueline Woodson, Kwame Alexander, and Sharon Draper. "If books that draw from our country and world's diversity are made available and are marketed the way books that are considered 'mainstream' are, they will do well."

Children's publishing is starting to catch up to what the Hudsons pioneered with Just Us. But just because things have improved doesn't mean it's time to stop. "Those of us who have, for years, been in the forefront of the movement for diversity, equity, and inclusion in children's literature, and those who have joined us, must continue to push and advocate," said Wade. "There still is much more work to be done."

Notes on Camp

Summer camp books are hardly an '80s phenomenon. At least since *Laura's Luck*, Marilyn Sach's 1965 tale of an urban bookworm's summer trip to the sticks, summer camp has been an archetypal YA and middle grade experience (and also a great place for teen characters to get a job—see page 152). In just one five-year stretch Ellen Conford's *Hail, Hail Camp Timberwood* (1978), Jane O'Connor's *Yours Till Niagara Falls, Abby* (1979), Gordon Korman's *I Want to Go Home* (1981), and eventual *Baby-Sitters Club* mastermind Ann M. Martin's first book, *Bummer Summer* (1983) were published, all of which helped establish the major plot conventions of camp books, i.e., the kid who's resistant to going to camp is initially fearful, then finally makes some friends, gets out of their social comfort zone, and grows as a person thanks to good times had in the Crafts Hut. In *Bummer*, for instance, 12-year-old Kammy reluctantly ships off to Camp Arrowhead because she can't get along with her new stepfamily. While there, she makes new friends, antagonizes a bully, learns to face her fears, and realizes she will come home a better person, changed in the way that only using an outhouse for several weeks can change you.

The fact that so much of camp lit is based on things that can only really happen to a person once is probably why just a handful of authors have been bold enough to

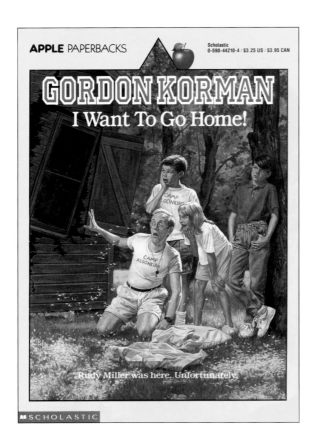

APPLE PAPERBACKS

Scholastic
0-590-44210-4 / $3.25 US / $3.95 CAN

GORDON KORMAN
I Want To Go Home!

CAMP ALGONKIAN

Rudy Miller was here. Unfortunately.

SCHOLASTIC

set a whole series there. Among those few chronic campers are the stars of Marilyn Kaye's Camp Sunnyside Friends series, which kept the girls of Cabin Six in action for twenty volumes between 1989 and 1992. Because everyone at Camp Sunnyside knows each other and the camp itself, there's no mystery about whether things will work out; the girls of Cabin Six, with their well-defined archetypes, fit in neatly with your babysitters, sleepover-ers, and girl talkers. They aren't scared to go to camp, they're excited about dealing with a whole new social landscape, and they most definitely don't utilize the fluid nature of the camp experience to reinvent themselves. Nope, they just ride horses, play color war, eventually learn that all boys aren't yucko, and so on. It's all stuff that, honestly, they could have also done at home—but, as in many tween books, the window dressing makes all the difference.

There's No "I" In Team

In the real world, women's sports rarely get media coverage on par with that of men's, but in girls' novels, they've been getting their due for longer than you might think. The Girls of Central High hit up a bunch of different extracurricular sports, and Jane Allen, heroine of her eponymous 1917 series by Edith Bancroft, played college basketball, which was especially cutting-edge considering the sport had only been around since 1891. That said, and despite the fact that 1972's Title IX required schools to provide female athletes with the same resources as their male peers, the '80s series boom was slow to feature sports outside stereotypically "female" disciplines like cheerleading, gymnastics, and ballet.

But boy, did those three get attention. The Cheerleaders series ran from 1985 to 1988, starring a squad of all the usual series suspects: the sassy one, the one who doesn't want anyone to know her family is actually broke, the one who is super-serious and focused because she used to be terribly sick, the mean girl who thirsts for sweet revenge against the protagonists, and, of course, the hot guy who would be perfect for our heroine except that he's too poor (?!). Through a remarkable forty-seven volumes, the gang struggled through questions of jealousy, familial discord, and sports ethics, digging a little deeper rather than just *rah-rah-rah*ing along. Many Cheerleaders authors went on to become big names in YA, including Caroline Cooney (see page 175). Even horror king Christopher Pike (see page 226) contributed Cheerleaders #2: *Getting Even* in 1985 (despite the fairly ominous title, nothing Pike-esque happens to the squads).

Cheerleading may have been an American teen sport since time immemorial (okay, actually since at least 1877, but the first women weren't allowed to participate until 1923), but gymnastics didn't take off as a typically tween pursuit until after the 1972 Olympics, when Soviet teen Olga Korbut transformed the sport from glorified

GETTING EVEN

Will jealousy tear them apart?

CHRISTOPHER PIKE

Most of the forty-seven
Cheerleaders titles alluded
to intense drama, athletic
competition, or both—to wit,
Splitting (#6), *Playing Games*
(#9), *All or Nothing* (#39)—but
its final title, *Dating* (#47) is
blissfully literal. The Gymnasts,
meanwhile, skewed a bit more
wholesome, and concluded the
series with *Go For the Gold: A
Gymansts Olympic Special*.

#7 **TUMBLING GHOSTS**

Elizabeth Levy

dance aerobics into a flashy, acrobatic crowd-pleasing performance. By the time 16-year-old American Mary Lou Retton won the all-around gold medal at the 1984 Olympics, gymnastics had become a full-blown tween obsession. So when the 1988 Olympics in Seoul rolled around, author Elizabeth Levy was ready. Over the course of four years, her Gymnasts series followed four tween gymnasts of varying ability, all of whom are members of the Pinecones, the beginner's team at Evergreen Gymnastics Academy. They each carry their own baggage: a fiery temper, a mother who was a gymnastics star, a famous dad whose celebrity causes others to treat her differently. They learn, they grow, they wear hot dog costumes, they eventually figure out how to get along with an 8-year-old gymnastics prodigy. As someone who was into gymnastics mostly because I liked playing with the chalk, I can't speak to whether their descriptions of landing jumps and flips are accurate. But they certainly are entertaining, and they provided the kind of wish fulfillment an average tween tumbler would have been eager to devour between practices.

Finally, there was ballet. Many series included characters who had a pair of toe shoes lying around, but Jahnna N. Malcolm's Bad News Ballet series, which debuted in 1989, put dance front and center in its tales of a group of mismatched weirdos, including a nerd, a fish out of water, and a vaguely butch tomboy, who must fight a group of wealthy and far more polished rivals for ballet supremacy.

APPLE PAPERBACKS
Scholastic 0-590-41916-1 / $2.50 US / $3.50 CAN

Bad News Ballet

#2 Battle of the Bunheads

OUR SIDE   DUMB SIDE!

Those snobs have gone too far this time!

Jahnna N. Malcolm

SCHOLASTIC

It's a classic snobs vs. slobs narrative, this time transposed onto the world of dance classes—which, at a time when girls of all different backgrounds were joining the once-rarified world of ballet, was a particularly hot commodity.

But not all girl-heavy sports involve sparkles, leotards, and hair-spraying your ponytail into a bun hard enough to inflict blunt trauma. Some instead involve stinky barns, special pants, and smacking giant animals on the butt with a crop! I speak, of course, of the equestrian arts. As someone who has never gone through a horse phase, I'm reluctant to even try to write about these series; the bond between a real woman and a fictional horse is intense and remains intrinsically mysterious to outsiders (even us outsiders who really, really tried to get into Breyer figurines in fifth grade). The power of this bond explains why horse books for children have been published virtually nonstop for the past 150 years, from *Black Beauty* in 1877, to early series like Billy and Blaze, the Black Stallion, and Misty of Chincoteague, whose first books were published in the '30s and '40s.

In the late '80s, that lineage begat Bonnie Bryant's Saddle Club, which along with Baby-Sitters **Club** and Sweet Valley High is one of the most iconic girls' series of the '80s and '90s. Much early horse lit had focused on either intense thoroughbred racing, wild horses, or farm animals, but this series prettied up the equine novel with riding lessons, little bows, and French-braided manes to create maximum appeal for yuppie offspring. After launching in 1988, the Saddle Club let readers gallop along with riders Carole, Stevie, and Lisa for 102 volumes, plus Super Editions, the spin-off series Pine Hollow (which follows the Saddle Club girls as older teens), and a younger readers' series, Pony Tails. While BSC reigned supreme by feeding reader fantasies of friendship (and, okay, a *tiny* bit of power) and Sweet Valley earned obsessive fans with its shameless drama, Saddle Club got to the top by nailing the horse girl ideal.

Of course, some of the major middle-grade-series tropes show up—Stevie is the tomboy, Lisa is the type A, Veronica is the rich mean girl, and the books' messages emphasized believing in yourself, caring about your friends, and handling tragedy. Still, horses are no mere garnish to help this series stand out from others—horses and horseback riding are its heart. Case in point: Carole, the third member of the Saddle Club, doesn't fit neatly into your classic '80s middle grade series molds because her "thing" is . . . she's a talented, dedicated rider. In the world of the Saddle Club, that's a trait that can help shape your identity, sense of yourself, and relationships with others as much as "being super-organized" or "hating 'girly' stuff" or any of those other tween archetypes.

Saddle Club ran for well over a decade, outlasting similarly themed competitor series like Chris St. John's Blue Ribbon (1989), Elizabeth Lindsay's Midnight Dancer (1993–97), Jeanne Betancourt's Pony Pals (1995–2003), and Joanna Campbell's Thoroughbred (1991–2005), which, at seventy-two volumes plus spin-offs, is nothing to sneeze at. But Saddle Club's lasting popularity isn't due just to the idea that some girls just really love horses—though some girls do *really* love horses, and Saddle Club is the only major series to convey how wonderful it feels to connect with animals, especially at an age when human relationships often become fraught and confusing. But the books also get the ecosphere of tween obsession right, utterly nailing the way an activity can connect with your heart and

soul and become the only pursuit that matters.

As the '90s began, series books finally began to routinely portray girls playing sports that had been traditionally considered for
boys. Girls playing "boy" sports had come up in earlier teen and
tween novels, but most of these early examples involved the athlete learning to act like a lady. For example, in 1989, Sweet Valley
Twins #89: *Standing Out* featured softball star Billie, who learns
that everyone (including her parents) like her more after she gets
a femme-y makeover and starts referring to herself as "Belinda."
Thankfully, such compulsory femininity barely figured into Lucy
Ellis's Pink Parrots series, published by Sports Illustrated for Kids
from 1990 to 1991. This six-book series followed the exploits of the
extremely ragtag all-girls baseball team the Pink Parrots, who
formed after pitcher Breezy became despondent over the way she
was treated as a member of the boys' team. Pink Parrots is mostly
about trying to fit a girls' sports narrative into the girls' series mold,

so its characterizations aren't exactly groundbreaking: we have the tomboy! The grouchy one! The ballerina who would rather be dancing! But it also engages with practical issues that come up in the lives of baseball-loving girls, including adults who refuse to make the most of their talents and dudes who say things like, "Girls who want to play baseball just want to be boys." The series also offers useful tips on how to be a good sport after you kick a sexist boy's ass so hard he's just about crying to his mama, which hopefully got some real-world application by readers.

Despite being praised by *Publishers Weekly* for its "catchy title, splashy cover and colorful cast of characters," the magazine's prediction that the Pink Parrots was "likely to be a hit" was, sadly, not in the (baseball) cards for these sluggers.

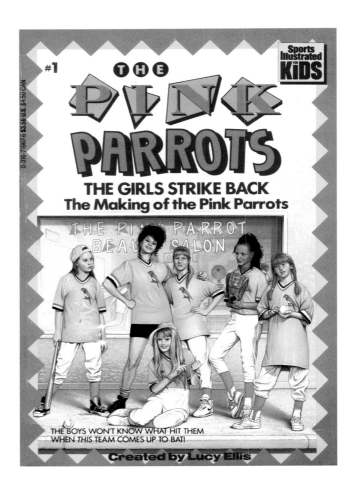

Pals Just Being Pals

By the late '80s, books about friendship for its own sake had become rare and were less popular than series featuring some kind of gimmick. But series about friendship and friendship alone *did* have the advantage of more space to experiment with concepts outside the YA mainstream than their hemmed-in, schtick-ridden fellows.

In many ways, the girls of Nicole Grey's 1993–94 series Girl Friends fit into the YA archetypes we've seen before: Cassandra's the ballet dancer, Maria is the popular cheerleader, Natalie is the one who used to live in the city, granola-chompin' activist Janis is the Dawn Schafer of the group. But the series combines all this with an ethnically and economically diverse group of girls and social issues. The girl friends of Girl Friends first connect in *Draw the Line*,

at a rally in response to gun violence, which helps confirm that we're not in Stoneybrook anymore (tragically, this remains a relevant scenario for teenagers). So do the presence of Stephanie Ling, the rare YA heroine whose family relies on her to work long post-school shifts to keep them economically stable, and plotlines about drug-addicted boyfriends, absentee fathers, and abusive relationships. Not to say that the series was perfectly sensitive or never presented any cringe-worthy moments. For instance, Natalie didn't come from just any city, she lived in Los Angeles, which

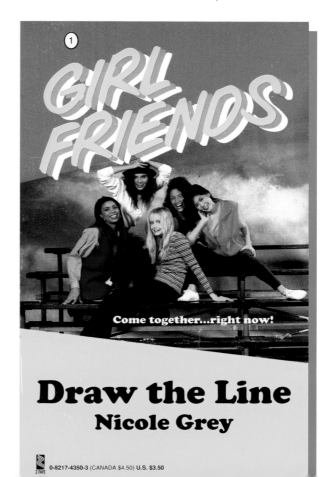

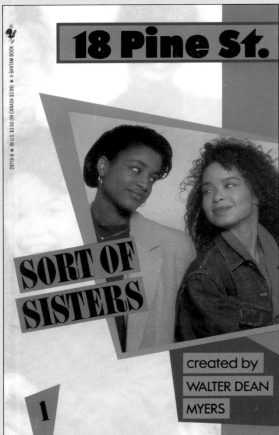

she fled following the 1992 riots, and she is first introduced tucking her hair into an "X" baseball cap and rapping along with "Baby Got Back." (Yeesh.) Still, the Girl Friends enjoyed typical moments of teen frivolity—writing school paper advice columns, going on fun dates, shopping, and crushing out on dudes who play in bands. Thus this series proved that the girls who populate serious "issue novels" and the girls who want to look cute at the school dance are, in fact, the same girls. Girls, and the Girl Friends, contain multitudes.

In some cases, the mere existence of a series could be quietly revolutionary. Though diversity in YA improved somewhat in '80s and '90s YA, racial representations were still incredibly far from equal, and people of color most commonly turned up in a series as a member of a predominantly white group (see: Claudia Kishi) or as part of a historical or issues novel specifically about racism. (Not to mention that many of those books were written by white authors.) The 18 Pine Street series, created by YA legend Walter Dean Myers, was one of the first teen series from a major publisher to focus on African American characters. Over the course of twelve volumes published from 1992 to 1994, the series followed the lives of a group of friends who hang out at 18 Pine (a pizza restaurant—don't let the outdoorsy name fool you). Relatable Sarah, sad rich girl Jennifer, orphan Tasha, cute nerd Kwame, and the rest of the group meet up after class to grab a few slices and chat about classic YA problems, like boyfriend-stealing classmates, false accusations of cheating on a test, competitive frenemies, or the logistics of throwing an enormous rager while your parents are away. Though the mainstream conversation about representation in children's literature had yet to hit its peak, these characters reflected a life that many tweens lived but that few got to see on the page.

Some authors took the friends-just-hangin'-out series model and gave it the mildest of twists, like Candice F. Ransom's Kobie Roberts books, straightforward and fairly timeless tales of friendship that happened to be set in the '60s (a fact totally not represented

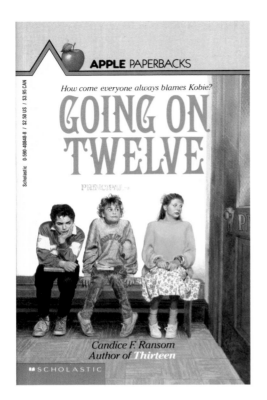

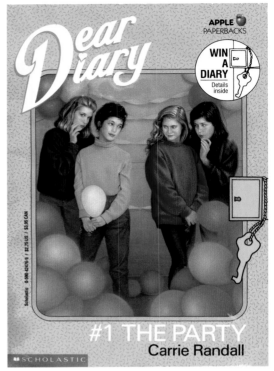

by the extremely '80s fashion on the covers, but a fact nonetheless!). Others dolloped on a heavier schmear of schtick, such as Carrie Randall in her six-book Dear Diary series, which ran from 1989 to 1991 and used first-person diary entries to make gentle examinations of tween girlhood a little snazzier (not to mention an illustrated lock and key on the edge of each volume's cover, to drive home the theme). Lizzie and Nancy, the sixth-grade protagonists, get on each other's nerves after spending too much time together, have trouble reading, and agonize over whether or not to go to the school dance. It's fairly mundane, but the same could be said of sixth grade. And some friendship series played it entirely straight, like Susan Smith's Best Friends series, which debuted in 1988. As the title implies, this series covered a group of best friends who hang for sixteen volumes' worth of adventures. But what the series lacked for gimmickery, it clearly made up for with drama and intrigue, as

Linda's running for class president... until the blackmail notes begin!

#13 Who's Out To Get Linda?
Susan Smith

Besides the 16 books in the Best Friends series, which follow nothing more supernatural than the petty dramas of junior high, Susan Smith also got a little ghoulish in the Samantha Slade: Monster Sitter series (see page 147).

evidenced by the title of installment #13, *Who's Out to Get Linda?* (One wonders what blackmail-able skeletons a preteen would have in her closet, but who knows, maybe she's a murderer—kids grow up earlier and earlier these days!)

The parade of endless gimmicks in friendship books may make all of them look hacky, but if anything, they confirm that (female) friendship is almost endless in its permutations, perennially intriguing, and always worthy of yet another series.

Frenemies 4 Ever

As we've established, '70s YA was about messiness, complexity, and complication, and '80s YA turned the tide toward the aspirational. But some '80s books still dared to admit that friendships can suck a big one.

To adults who devote their mental bandwidth to extremely mature concerns like whether to get a "smart thermostat," YA friendship dramas can feel impossibly distant and/or trivial. But some teenage situations remain relatable for the rest of your life, such as when your best friend gets a new friend you *can. not. stand.* This eternal dilemma is at the core of Sheila Hayes's 1986 novel *You've Been Away All Summer*, a surprisingly sophisticated story about evolving friendships. Sarah and Fran have been best friends since first grade—"up until then, in nursery school and kindergarten, we

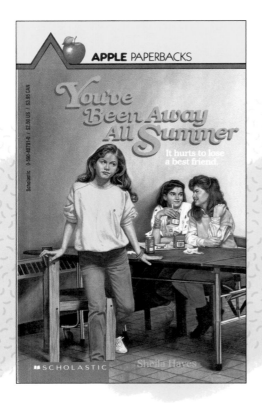

traveled in different crowds"—but in the titular summer before seventh grade, Fran leaves town for two months and Sarah lands a new BFF, the dreaded Marcie. Marcie is rude, irresponsible, in love with a boy who tortures cats, and, in one scene, shockingly racist! The book perfectly captures Sarah's befuddlement as she tries to understand what it means for her best friend to love this terrible, irritating idiot. Although Sarah and Marcie's disagreements about appropriate behavior at the natural history museum are (hopefully) of limited use to adult readers, Hayes's portrait of the fears and oversensitivity present in a shifting friendship remains weirdly (perhaps depressingly) relevant.

Natalie Honeycutt's *Invisible Lissa* from 1985 delves into another friendship concern: what happens when a terrible, toxic person worms into your social circle. Debra is not just popular, pushy, and into stealing people's jumbo novelty pens; she's also a power-mad lunatic who founds the unappetizingly named FUNCHY Club (it stands for "Fun Lunch," obviously) as a cudgel to destroy her enemies—which includes Lissa after she is caught gossiping about Debra at the class Valentine's Day party. Suddenly Debra is smashing Lissa's class project, picking fights with Lissa's brother who is literally a toddler, and getting all the other girls in class to turn on her, *Crucible*-style. *Lissa* is interesting less for the specifics of its plot (Lissa undertakes a fairly standard middle grade spiritual journey, learning to find worth within herself rather than in invites to funch) than for its examination of the sociopathic underpinnings of a YA character's drive for popularity. Viewed from a different angle, Debra would probably look like a tween romance novel heroine, dressed in the newest fashions and hell-bent on social supremacy. But in *Lissa*, she's revealed for what she is: an annoying jerk who picks fights with toddlers.

Surprisingly, "nice girl befriends borderline sociopath" was a well-populated category of tween novel. Even paranormal queen Betty Ren Wright got in on the action—when she wasn't

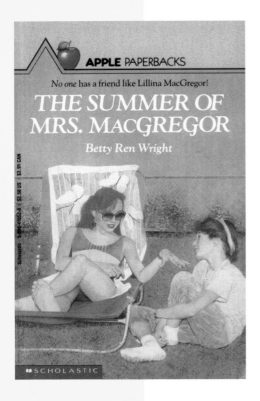

documenting the special relationship between spunky teenage girls and helpful wraiths (see page 219), she also took occasional stabs at ghost-free realism. In her 1986 book *The Summer of Mrs. MacGregor*, Caroline Cabot is 12 years old and having a grim summer—her older sister Linda is critically ill, she's stuck at home with her father while her mother is off helping Linda get treatment, her job's a bummer—until the arrival of Lillina Taylor MacGregor. Lillina is either a wealthy, married 17-year-old model/photographer who's hanging around the Midwestern suburbs for kicks *or* a 15-year-old who deals with her unsatisfying home life by lying about living in New York, being married, and working for *Vogue* (and also by stealing any money she sees lying around). No spoilers about which is true, but the same empathy Wright brings to the tortured heroines of her supernatural novels pops up here, applied to both narcissistic Lillina and self-conscious Caroline.

Some not-quite-friends stories (admittedly, relatively few) drew upon characters' disparate backgrounds to create tension. Alice Larsen, the heroine of Marie G. Lee's 1993 book *If It Hadn't Been for Yoon Jun*, is of Korean heritage but was adopted by white American parents as an infant and considers their culture her own. She's resistant to her parents' encouragement to learn more about Korean culture and irritated when they suggest she get to know unpopular Yoon Jun, a boy who recently moved to their town from Korea. But a school project about their birth country brings the pair together, and Alice learns not only about Korean culture, but also about treating people with respect (aka exactly the opposite of what her popular-crowd buddies are doing). Lee, founder of the Asian American Writers' Workshop, wrote a novel for adults about transracial adoption, *Somebody's Daughter*, in 2005 as Marie Myung-Ok Lee, and her work is some of the first to straddle the ever-thinning line between YA and "prestigious" literature (see sidebar, page 36).

But the ultimate X factor in "are we friends or do I actually hate your guts" situations is, naturally, hormonally charged mixed romantic signals in opposite-sex friendships. In Dean Marney's 1989 novel *You, Me, and Gracie Makes Three*, Rick and Linda are best friends, even though Linda is a pretentious aspiring artist who swans around in serapes and Rick, well, likes basketball. They seem to hate each other, but is the hate just a cover for something more? The answer turns out to be yes: Linda is in love with Rick and Rick can't deal, until they have a life-changing experience with a wise, eccentric elderly person named Gracie (making this

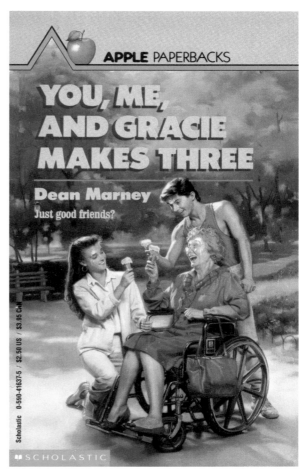

Scholastic 0-590-41637-5 / $2.50 US / $3.95 CN

basically an unauthorized remake of *The Pigman* by Paul Zindel, the definitive YA text on having your life changed by a wacky elderly person, but with less depth and a happier ending).

However thorny the frenemyship in these novels, most stay *just* on the safe side of "problem lit." But a rarefied few touched on actual life-and-death matters, including Ann M. Martin's extremely dark novel *Slam Book*. Before we had secret social media accounts we could use to talk smack about our high school classmates without repercussion, slam books—notebooks in which you wrote anonymous gossip about your peers—were quite the sensation, especially in the pages of YA. Slam books catalyzed the action of Judy Blume's 1972 novel *Otherwise Known as Sheila the Great*, provided a crucial weapon in the war against Taffy Sinclair (as we've seen on page 53), and swept through the halls of Sweet Valley High in 1988 (#48: *Slam Book Fever*). In Martin's novel, Anna decides she'll make a slam book to up her social status because, hey, destroying other people psychologically is the best way to become popular in high school. At first, it works: she gets in with the in crowd and is even able to date a cute guy thanks to a slam-book-induced breakup. But slam-book-based happiness isn't meant to last, and soon tempers flare, Anna and her friends start writing mean things about each other in the book, a slam-book-based prank on an unpopular classmate leads to that girl's suicide—and then one of Anna's friends *also* attempts suicide! Anna's friend is saved, everyone eventually repents, and they throw the book away, vowing never again to collect cruel anonymous gossip (No one is punished for taunting a girl who ended her life, but maybe that's realism for you.) Sure, *Slam Book* is melodramatic, but it also provides a nice rejoinder to baby boomers wailing that the internet is turning innocent kids into vicious bullies. Au contraire; we've been monsters all along.

Scholastic 0-590-41838-6 / $2.75 US / $3.95 CAN

SLAM BOOK

*You can write anything
in a slam book...
no matter
who it hurts*

Ann M. Martin
author of
Missing Since Monday

■ SCHOLASTIC

CHAPTER 3

Family

KID BROTHERS,

SNOTTY SISTERS,

and

GOOD OL' MOM

AND DAD

FRANCINE PASCAL'S

38

SWEET VALLEY HIGH

SWITZE

Can Jessica find a way to stop Elizabeth from leaving Sweet Valley?

LEAVING HOME

I n 1986, Ronald Reagan—onetime star of *Cattle Queen of Montana*, now the president of the United States— declared that "in recent decades, the American family has come under virtual attack." Such was the prevailing conservative moral panic thought at the time: the cultural changes of the '60s and '70s had ruined everyone's lives, single and working mothers were a blight on society, and America's children could be saved from lives of desperation only if everyone agreed to some serious *Leave It to Beaver* role-playing.

Families *were* changing, however. Developments in and shifting attitudes about birth control during the sexual revolution, plus a mild recession, had put a dent in procreation; in the mid-1970s, the average birth rate plunged from its mid-1950s peak to the lowest of the century, less than two children per woman. Meanwhile, the divorce rate had more than doubled between 1960 and 1980— catalyzed, in part, by the nation's first no-fault divorce bill in 1969, signed into law in California by . . . governor Ronald Reagan. Whoops! All told, about half of children born in the 1970s to married couples would see their parents split up.

YA lit, too, was dealing with the double standards and tangled values of the changing American family. After decades of portraying idealized parents in malt shop books and Nancy Drew mysteries, YA in the '70s had leaned hard into parents who were, as then *New York Times* children's book editor Julie Just wrote in 2010, "ineffectual, freaked out, self-centered, losing it." But in the '80s, YA widened its scope to include all kinds of families with all kinds of problems, including what Beth Nelms and Ben Nelms describe in their 1984 *English Journal* article "Ties that Bind Families in YA Books" as "happy stories of warm families, realistic stories of normal tensions and adjustments, stories that deal fairly with children estranged from their parents, and powerful stories of the dark and glorious strains of family history." Some books documented troubled families under tremendous stress; others tried to comfort kid readers by normalizing the experience of watching parents divorce, date, or remarry. Some positioned the family as the only safe harbor from our unsympathetic garbage barge of a world. Some let the timeless struggles of sibling drama rule the stage. And some simply used the family as a pro forma setting (since 10-year-olds generally live with other people). But all in all, these books resisted hollow "family values" rhetoric by demonstrating the value in depicting actual families.

Irreconcilable Differences

Divorce in YA had hit the mainstream as early as Judy Blume's 1972 book *It's Not the End of the World*, but by the early '80s, YA divorce lit had grown into a full-on microgenre. Split parents became as ubiquitous in tween fiction as crimped hair or irritating younger siblings. Everyone and their mother (literally) was getting divorced.

Early YA divorce classics like Paula Danziger's 1982 novel *The Divorce Express* established many soon-to-be-common themes. As heroine Phoebe, who shuttles between her artsy dad and more traditional mom, puts it: "I have to learn how to handle this new situation so that it works out well for me—as well as it can without being really what I want." With that insight gained, her transition to the child who is now wiser than her divorced parents is complete.

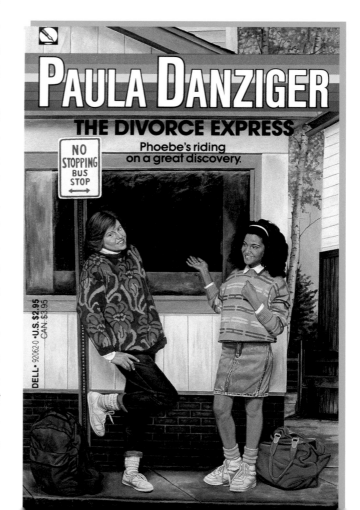

Subsequent books dug into the logistical considerations of divorce: Which parent would you live with? (Judie Angell's 1981 novel *What's Best for You.*) How would you cope with having two homes? (Jeanne Betancourt's 1983 novel *The Rainbow Kid.*) If your dad remarries a much younger woman, will your mom lose it? (Norma Klein's 1984 novel *Angel Face.*) And if you're a young girl witnessing a nasty divorce, how are

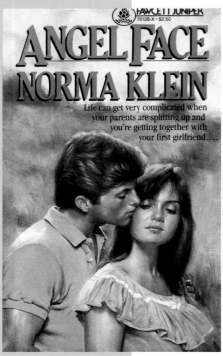

you supposed to ever trust men again?

Two middle-grade books tackled that last question: Betty Bates's *The Great Male Conspiracy* in 1986 and Anna Grossnickle Hines's *Boys Are Yucko!* in 1989. In *Boys*, fifth-grader Cassie lives with her newly single mom, awaiting some form of contact from her newly deadbeat dad; in *Conspiracy*, 12-year-old Maggie is reeling after her beloved older sister's husband, a dirtbag Stanley Kowalski type, leaves right after the birth of their child. In both, the girls wonder about these creatures called "men," and why so many otherwise sensible women want them in their lives. Is it a trick? Some kind of pyramid scheme? Cassie is appalled when the girls in her class want her to invite boys to her birthday party. Maggie's disgust is directed toward a dad who rarely helps with chores and her wiener-y friend Todd, who likes to put her down with oddly specific burns like, "You've been moping around for weeks, drooping like some flat tire."

By the end of their respective novels, both Maggie and Cassie decide that most guys are all right and should be evaluated on a case-by-case basis—a decision that's less a credit to the greatness of the men in their lives than a first foray into the timeless womanly art of settling.

A DELL YEARLING BOOK

DELL• 40247-6 •U.S. $2.95
CAN. $3.95

"Boys are infants. Boys never grow up. Never."

The Great Male Conspiracy

Betty Bates

The illustrations for both *The Great Male Conspiracy* and *Boys Are Yucko!* err on the side of "personal space invasion, but not in a *super* creepy way" with some halfhearted hair pulling and condescending head-patting.

APPLE PAPERBACKS

Scholastic
0-590-43109-9 / $2.75 US / $3.50 CAN

BOYS ARE YUCKO!

BOYS KEEP OUT!

Everybody's gone boy-crazy except Cassie!

Anna Grossnickle Hines

SCHOLASTIC

The Drama Doesn't Fall Far from the Tree

Divorcing parents may have inflicted some of the flashiest trauma in '80s and '90s teen lit, but they hardly had a monopoly on it. There were plenty of other ways for parents to stress their kids out! Sometimes, it was as simple as possessing a unique set of quirks and neuroses, as in Carol Snyder's 1983 novel *Memo: To Myself When I Have a Teenage Kid*, in which 13-year-old Karen is aggravated by her uncool mom until she uncovers her mom's adolescent diary and finds that even moms were once awkward, boy-crazy disasters. In Patricia MacLachlan's 1988 book *The Facts and Fictions of Minna Pratt*, a quirky writer-mom presides over a clan of oddballs akin to J. D. Salinger's Glass family who spend the novel

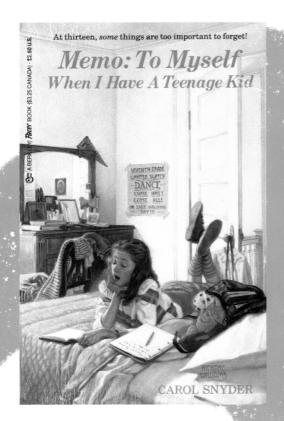

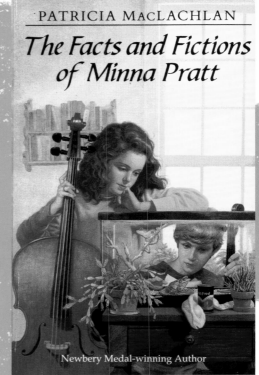

quirking around, trying to learn healthy boundaries in between whimsical bouts of humming (seriously). Audra Spotts's 1983 novel *Standing Ovation* wanders through similar territory, depicting a girl from a large family who decides to get her ex-musician father's attention by taking up an instrument herself.

Other parents put more effort into the low-key ruining of their child's life, such as those in Mitali Perkins's 1993 book *The Sunita Experiment.* Sunita Sen's parents upend her life when they hear that her maternal grandparents are coming from India for an extended stay at their California home. Crazed with her own residual adolescent insecurity, Sunita's mom rushes to present a more conventional front to her family, taking a leave of absence from her job as a chemistry teacher, wearing saris instead of pants, and switching out the family's takeout pizza for homemade

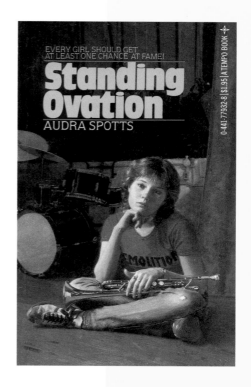

The cover of *The Sunita Experiment* is a rare example of a highly stylized cover—most books of this era sported photos or photorealistic illustrations. But that's not the only reason this cover is notable: it also portrays its heroine as the girl of color that she is, rather than "whitewash" (aka portray a nonwhite character with a white model or illustration) her, an unfortunate act of erasure that was known to plague (and still does) middle grade and YA covers.

School Library Journal praised *Goodbye, Pink Pig* as "a sensitive story" that "should appeal to children who have suffered from the 'lonelies'" (which, honestly, is a lot of them).

Indian foods. Sunita initially responds by withdrawing socially, confident that neither her friends nor the boy she loves would want to deal with her "weird" family." But eventually, multiple generations of the Sen family learn that embracing your weirdness is kind of what life is about. *Sunita* is remarkable not just for flipping the script and making the mom the awkward, insecure child character; it also engages with the struggle of relating to two cultures at once, at a time when such depictions were relatively rare.

In general, the parents in '80s and '90s tween lit were more well-adjusted than their '70s counterparts. But not every book in this era was about families of shiny, happy people holding hands. The hostile, self-centered, traumatizing parents of YA's golden age still turned up, in books like C. S. Adler's *Good-Bye Pink Pig* from 1985, a sort of middle grade *Glass Menagerie*, complete with the brother who suddenly leaves home, the mother with impossible expectations, and the young woman who takes solace in some friendly knickknacks. Ten-year-old Amanda has a hard time at school and also at home, where her unkind, unhinged, wealth-obsessed mother berates her kids and refuses to let them speak to their paternal grandmother, who has a blue-collar job. To cope, Amanda loses herself inside a fantasy world inhabited by her favorite crystal pig figurine and other assorted trinkets (because who wouldn't?). But in a significant departure from Tennessee Williams, Amanda gets a happy ending, living with her doting grandmother as her mother departs for a new life where, one hopes, she can maybe figure out her issues.

Judy Blume also got into the complicated world of depressed, confused parents, in one of her rare '80s works. For an author that many instantly associate with the '80s, Blume in fact published most of her famous fiction in the '70s. Her fiction output for this decade comprised *Superfudge*, the 1980 sequel to *Tales of a Fourth Grade Nothing*; the friendship novel *Just as Long as We're Together* in 1987; and *Tiger Eyes*, in 1981, in the middle.

Of her three '80s titles, *Tiger Eyes* covers the most classic Blume turf. After her father is murdered at her family's New Jersey convenience store, 15-year-old Davey Wexler can barely get out of bed. Her equally depressed mom decides the family should take a short trip to New Mexico to visit Davey's Aunt Bitsy and Uncle Walter, which turns into a year-long stay. Surrounded by desert and living under the legacy of the atom bomb (Walter works at Los Alamos), Davey begins to engage with the world again, befriending a local

Is Davey strong enough to
put the pieces of her world
back together?

Tiger Eyes

DELL · 98469 · 2.50

LAUREL-LEAF BOOKS

Judy Blume

girl named Jane as well as a mysterious boy named Wolf. Through volunteering at a local hospital, where she learns that Wolf is also trying to cope with family trauma, Davey comes back to life and pushes back against her PTSD; eventually, she's able to part with the blood-stained clothes that she wore as she held her dying father and begin to move on.

Though *Tiger Eyes* never explicitly comes out in opposition to family values rhetoric (which, in 1981, had barely started to gather critical mass), it takes a definitive stance against the kind of sheltering, "father knows best" parenting that Reaganite culture advocated for—Bitsy and Walter are obsessed with safety (they don't want Davey to take driving lessons because they think it's dangerous) and conventional metrics of success like good grades. Davey and her mother's recovery crystallizes only when they can push back against Walter and Bitsy and return to New Jersey to live their messy, complicated, *real* lives.

Non-Novel Spin-Offs

Sometimes, following the fictional adventures of problematic yet beloved '80s characters in novels wasn't enough for audiences. Sometimes, characters broke the literary fourth wall and addressed real readers directly, in the weirdest form of series spin-off: the nonfiction companion book!

Although the idea of squeezing eager tween consumers for everything they've got with barely related ancillary titles feels like something Jessica and Elizabeth would have pioneered, these books existed in the earliest days of the '80s romance boom; in 1981, Judy Blume released a tie-in diary called, appropriately, *The Judy Blume Diary*, which was marketed as a "special place to write about your very special feelings" and which could be purchased via a coupon in the back of books like *Tiger Eyes*. Two years later, Bantam published the advice volume *How to Talk to Boys (and Other Important People)*, which offered readers of the Sweet Dreams series such crucial advice as "The Best Time to Call a Boy" ("Think twice about calling him the night before a big final or the evening before term papers are due.") and "Dealing with his Criticism" ("By never questioning Nick's hurtful remarks, Nell contributed to the problem.").

The Wakefields quickly got in on the act, offering books seemingly aimed at helping the reader become a shallow, catty weirdo who places unnecessary strain on all of her personal relationships with a bottomless need for pointless drama. I am speaking, of course, about the 1988 *Sweet Valley High Slam Book*. Sold as a riff on installment #48, *Slam Book Fever*, the book was divided into categories like "Biggest Flirt," "Most Likely to Have Six Kids," and "Most Like Elizabeth Wakefield," so that you too

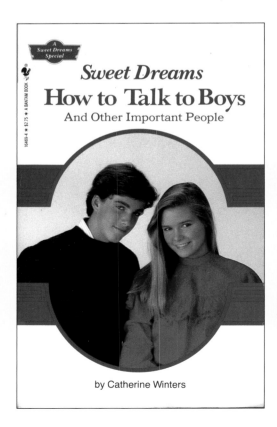

by Catherine Winters

could anonymously insult your friends via a notebook that they all saw you writing in. Naturally, copies of this companion title now sell for about $1,000 on eBay.

If your parents deemed you too young for a mass-produced burn book, you could still get your hands on the 1990 *Sweet Valley Twins Super Summer Fun Book*, which, you'll be happy to hear, was just as bizarre. The book is filled with tips about how to run a social club like the Unicorns ("Dues: The Unicorns each pay a dime every week. You can use the club money to throw parties, go on trips, or buy materials for special club projects") and how to curl your hair with pipe cleaners, as well as horoscopes to help you figure out why the universe cursed you to worship these monster-girls and the Fiat they rode in on.

Obsessive Baby-Sitters Club fans who wanted to wear Kristy's skin like a hat got a weird spin-off in 1991 in the form of the *Baby-Sitters Club Notebook*, which taught readers the ancient art of babysitting, complete with sections on emergency care, tips for finding clients, and blank notebook pages in the back so that you could experience the thrill of . . . owning a book that was only 80 pages long but felt like an even 100.

This last feature is emblematic of most nonfiction spin-offs; they delivered all of the brand awareness with around 40 percent of the content but 100 percent of the list price. Seems like a naked cash grab, but their insights were at least *trying* to be helpful. And who knows, maybe Nick and Nell are happily married to this day.

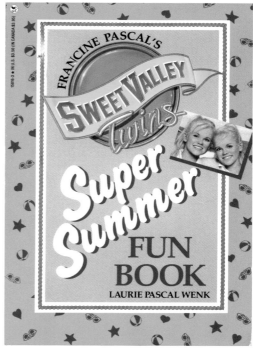

Sister, Sister (or Possibly Brother)

Though parents sometimes fade into the background of a YA novel, siblings rarely do—perhaps because they're just so damned annoying. Even before the YA genre had a name, countless books for younger readers, like Laura Ingalls Wilder's Little House books and Sydney Taylor's All-of-a-Kind Family series, turned heavily on the joys and sorrows of life with siblings. But in the '80s and '90s, even that most basic childhood relationship transformed into something of a gimmick.

Friends, what can I possibly say that hasn't already been said about Jessica and Elizabeth Wakefield, the First Siblings of '80s teen fiction? Part of a weird kid-lit fixation on twins that long predated even the Bobbsey Twins, these Fiat-drivin', size-6-wearin' gals from Sweet Valley were the brainchild of Francine Pascal, who by the time she created the series had already written several well-received YA novels (see page 33), as well as scripts for a soap opera called *The Young Marrieds*. But Pascal was done with "well-received." She conceived of the Wakefields as nothing short of a force for world domination—i.e., the series was ghostwritten from the get-go. As Pascal told the *Guardian* in 2012: "I wanted this to be read by a bigger audience. The books I had written before . . . were for a more sophisticated, educated audience. But I wanted Sweet Valley to be for everyone." What a self-own, Francine! And yet, despite this careful engineering for mass appeal and productions, the series was originally intended to include only six books.

Was there a hint in book #1: *Double Love*, in 1983, as we were introduced to gorgeous, wealthy blonde twins—one boring, the other sociopathic—that they would become our constant cultural companions for the next fifteen years? As the sisters first fought over stupid Todd, was there an inkling that Sweet Valley High would become the first YA series to hit the *New York Times* adult best-seller list (in 1985, with the Super Edition *Perfect Summer*) and thereby usher children's literature into the realm of big business? As Jessica swanned around plotting to ruin her sister's life because a boy had the audacity to find Elizabeth more attractive, did we dare dream that this series might run for 143 volumes—plus miniseries, two separate prequel series for young readers, and something called magna editions (which I originally read as "manga editions," but which are actually just "extra-special" installments and not graphic novel treatments at all). As mean rich girl Lila Fowler inexplicably demanded to turn the school football field into a factory, could we have possibly guessed that twenty-nine years later, in 2011, we'd be lining up for *Sweet Valley Confidential*, a sequel that confirmed that all the characters experienced zero emotional growth in the decade since high school? In short: what the hell is wrong with us?

Francine Pascal once famously remarked that "I didn't intend Sweet Valley to be realistic," which I'd certainly hope! Sweet Valley books immediately stood apart from Judy Blume's tales of teen neuroses and other publishers' wholesome teen romances alike through their sheer over-the-top-ness. Throughout the series, Jessica (the evil, scheming twin who was always cheating on her boyfriends) and Elizabeth (the good, irritatingly self-righteous twin who nevertheless *also* cheated on her boyfriends) experienced a run of trauma that would send any other laid-back California babe running for the nearest sanitarium. One or both Wakefields: got lost at sea (the imaginatively titled #56:

Lost at Sea), were kidnapped by a cult (the imaginatively titled #82: *Kidnapped by the Cult!*), fell into a coma and then came out with a completely different personality (#7: *Dear Sister*), attempted to run away to Switzerland (#38: *Leaving Home*; see page 90), ostracized a classmate until she attempted suicide (#10: *The Wrong Kind of Girl*), killed the other twin's boyfriend via inadvertent drunk driving (#95: *The Morning After*, #96: *The Arrest*, and #97: *The Verdict*), and, perhaps most traumatically, dyed her hair black so that they no longer looked identical (#32: *The New Jessica*).

The absurdity that makes it so easy to goof on the Wakefields today is also probably what got us so invested in these two dunderheads when we were younger. In *Sisters, Schoolgirls, and Sleuths*, children's literature expert Carolyn Carpan called Sweet Valley the "first soap opera romance series" for teens, and indeed, the books privileged plot twists above realism. Pascal, who had once toyed with developing a TV soap for teens, conceived of each book as a stand-alone story that nonetheless invited the

FRANCINE PASCAL'S

SWEET VALLEY HIGH™

32

Elizabeth's twin has become a complete stranger!

THE NEW JESSICA

On the cover of book #32, *The New Jessica*, the Wakefields seem to take a page from those other icons of American feminine duality and fighting over boys, Archie Comics' Betty and Veronica. Jessica's "European" makeover makes her look a little more like the life-ruining vixen she always aspired to be (she even fakes a British accent!), but the brown hair is gone by the end of the book.

reader to continue to the next volume—a structure which played as much a role in the series' theatrical vibe as did the storylines. The Wakefields weren't so different from other romance heroines of the era, but what set them apart was the sheer speed at which life seemed to assail them with trials and tribulations.

And that speed was the recipe for success, according to Pascal. She once claimed that Harlequin romances were "slow" and that teenagers don't enjoy them or similar books because "nothing happens" in them. (So, in case you were wondering: Francine definitely seems like a Jessica.) Plus, the series was truly an ongoing story, and characters reappeared in book after book, unlike Sweet Dreams and other romances of the era (page 19), which presented one-off stories sewn up with a tight happily-ever-after at the end, no cliffhanger necessary. Also, even though they seemed to wake up every morning and immediately encounter a third twin hell-bent on their deaths, or whatever, the twins always looked good and acted cool. Jess and Liz were as far as you could get from a messy, confused problem-novel heroine while still being members of the same species. Pascal's girls had not only reshaped the romance boom, they had left the classic teen "issues" novel in the dust. As the author blithely told the *Chicago Tribune* in 1991, "on the whole, teenage life isn't about drug and pregnancies or rape. . . . It revolves more around virginal angst and first love, both of which are very serious subjects." Maybe. More likely, readers were using Sweet Valley as an escape from their distinctly non-Wakefieldian real lives.

More than anything, what set Sweet Valley High apart from other teen romances was that, at their core, they were about family. Sure, the stories were more often about plotting to steal someone's boyfriend or accidentally getting brainwashed than they were about analyzing the true meaning of the sisterly bond, but without the family dynamic, the rest would be for naught. Two teen friends trying to steal each other's boyfriends? Eh. Two *identical twins* trying to steal each other's boyfriends? Dude, that is straight-up disgusting, and weird, and upsetting, and I can't look away. Their family feuds are the real star of the show—we're here for the break-ups and makeups between Jessica and Elizabeth, not the ones they have with a bunch of faceless, interchangeable Chads. The twins' abrupt about-facing from jealous scheming to peaceful forgiveness was in itself a kind of escapism; countless series promised hot boys and dangerous, thrilling situations, but how many promised that your sister would endlessly put up with your nonsense, and do it with a smile? Now there's a fantasy.

In the rush to find the next Wakefields, some publishers took things pretty literally, pumping out stories of yet more identical twins who find themselves in even more dramatic, unbelievable mishaps. I assume this was the genesis of Charlotte St. John's Red Hair trilogy—though the 1989 series is closer to a dark *Parent Trap* rewrite than any kind of Wakefield pastiche. Wealthy teen Emily was raised to believe that her mother and twin sister Elaine were killed in a car accident when she was a baby, but she later finds out that in fact her parents divorced, and when they split, her father won full custody of both girls. Her mother kidnapped Elaine (but left baby Emily to just chill with her ex-husband), then faked both their deaths and fled across the country, as one does. But only for a decade or so, at which point she decided to give up the whole ruse because, hey, plot momentum! The twins reunite with much less fuss and legal intervention than you'd expect, given the circumstances, and split their time between their mother and father's homes while still making time for edgy delinquent boyfriends in the 1991 follow-up, *Red Hair, Too* and HIV awareness (but also boyfriends) one year later, in *Red Hair Three*. Emily and Elaine did not stand the test of time as well as the look-alikes from Sweet Valley did, nor did they necessarily push the envelope on important issues (though the series interjected a little diversity into the world of twin series; the girls have a white father and a Latina mother,

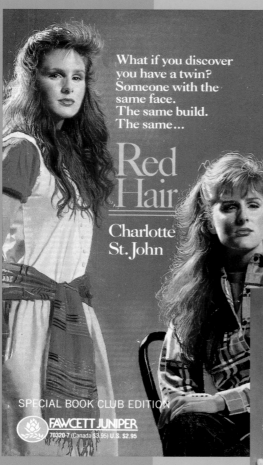

What if you discover
you have a twin?
Someone with the
same face.
The same build.
The same...

Red
Hair

Charlotte
St. John

SPECIAL BOOK CLUB EDITION

FAWCETT JUNIPER
70320-7 (Canada $3.95) U.S. $2.95

Though the tagline for *Red
Hair* pushes the "twin" aspect
preeeetty hard, the cover
design ditches the familiar
oval inset for a full-bleed
illustration, lest these new
twins on the block seem
too close to their blonde
Californian forbears.

FAWCETT JUNIPER
70392-4 (Canada $4.50) U.S. $3.50

Even after you find your twin,
there's still a lot to
learn about her....

Red Hair, Too

Charlotte St. John
Author of *RED HAIR*

a fact that is absolutely not reflected on the covers) but at least they didn't spend several pages in every book telling you how hot they were.

Identical twins didn't have a monopoly on stories about sisters fighting over awful boys, though the singleton sisters in Norma Fox Mazer's 1986 novel *Three Sisters* are not as eager to forgive and forget as the Wakefield sibs. The book could just as easily have been titled *Three Crappy Boyfriends*, because each sister has one: 15-year-old Karen has Davey, who relentlessly pressures her for sex and, after she refuses, drops her for her best friend; 18-year-old Tobi has Jason, her 30-something college art teacher who sculpts when he isn't busy being a violent drunk; and 21-year-old Liz has Scott, her fiancé, who flirts with the hopelessly crushed-out Karen . . . and then kisses her! On two separate occasions! While she's still 15! Mazer emphasizes how these problems, which initially place stress on the siblings' relationships with one another, ultimately pale before the strength of their bond. But the secondary story is about how even smart, confident women from loving, supportive families can end up in relationships with people who run the gamut from sleazy to criminal. So while the book offers a shot of hope, there's also a streak of darkness: strong family bonds cannot protect us completely from injurious outside forces, no matter what President Ronnie says.

I Guess We're Technically Related?

In addition to parent and sibling stories, in the '90s, the family novel spotlight briefly turned to cousins. Sibling books still reigned supreme, to be sure, but some publishers, burned out on the antics of the Wakefield sisters and various spooky psychic twins from teen horror novels, went in search of novelty. And for one brief, shining moment, they found it with the main character's mom's brother's daughters.

Cousin lit could be high-brow, as in award-winning author Virginia Hamilton's 1990 novel *Cousins*, in which Cammie has a complicated, prickly relationships with Patty Ann, her wealthy, perfectionist cousin who secretly struggles with an eating disorder. Cammie and Patty Ann's complex relationship continues on after Patty Ann's sudden death, eventually bringing the entire family

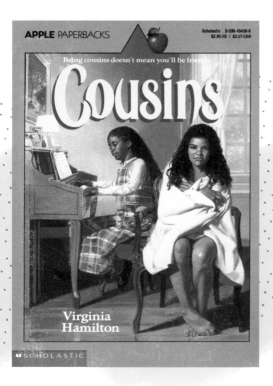

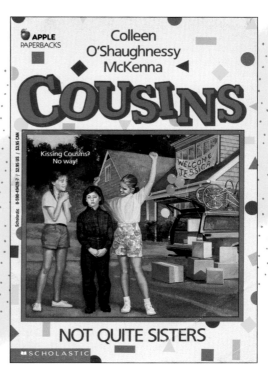

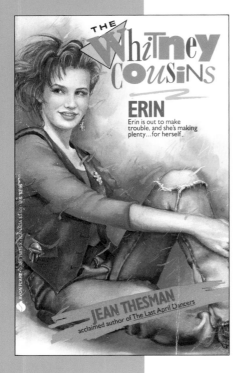

back together, including Cammie's dad, who's been out of the picture for a while.

But often, this subgenre was far more commercial, like Colleen O'Shaughnessy McKenna's Cousins series, which lasted for two volumes in the summer of 1993, perhaps because of its obvious and limited subject matter. Book #1, *Not Quite Sisters*, follows Callie, the eldest in a crew of six cousins, who is trying to welcome her cousin Jessica back to town. This in turn creates drama with another cousin, Lindsay, who is jealous of Jessica. For example: "Maybe you hang around with me because I'm the cousin closest to you in age. But, what if you decide Jessica is the *best* cousin?" In the next book, *Stuck in the Middle*, Lindsay and Jessica start to worry when Callie drops them for the group of older kids that hangs around the public pool. Publisher Apple seems to have realized that there's a ceiling on how much drama you can wring out of the relationships between people who have known one another their whole lives, but also who see each other twice a week tops, and bagged the enterprise fast. (Also, I'm not here to point fingers, but the tagline on *Not*

The Whitney Cousins covers made the family series a little funkier and jazzier for the '90s, complete with artistically torn-up jeans and a type treatment ripped from a Caboodle.

Quite Sisters, "Kissing cousins? No way!" seems to badly misunderstand *at least* two concepts.)

Slightly more successful was Jean Thesman's Whitney Cousins series, which totaled four books published between 1990 and 1992. The Whitneys didn't focus exclusively on cousin-on-cousin squabbling; these three cousin-friends dealt with extremely contemporary social issues like blended families, the death of a parent, sexual assault, and so on, all while wearing what your mom would call a "funky" outfit (as you can see on the opposite page, the girls were fond of statement brooches, sassy vests, and a nice gladiator sandal). Yet even that approach seemed to hit a wall awfully quickly, and after three books that examined weightier topics, we suddenly had #4: *Triple Trouble*, a book about the town carnival and one Whitney cousin's effort to become a clown. (Really, *we're* the clowns for having bought this stuff, right? Am I right? I'll show myself out.) Despite its best efforts to push the clown-containing envelope, cousin-core never took off the way books about closer blood ties managed to.

CHAPTER 4

School

CLASSMATES,

CAFETERIAS,

and

GROUP PROJECTS

GONE BAD

15

THE GIRLS OF CANBY HALL®

Who said being honest was easy?

TO TELL THE TRUTH

EMILY CHASE

Scholastic   0-590-33759-9 / $1.95

B etween the ages of 5 and 18, kids spend eight hours a day, five days a week, nine-ish months a year stuck in a building that smells like microwavable pizza and industrial tile cleaner. Frankly, it's tough to set a tween book anywhere else. But the sheer amount of time kids are legally required to be in school alone does not explain its incredible popularity as a YA setting. School also has all the ingredients necessary for a dramatic narrative baked right in: complex hierarchies, constant power struggles, being forced to interact with your enemies, and so on.

For an evergreen source of drama, school and schooling have changed a lot in the past century. In 1900, only about 50 percent of American children of any age, race, or gender were enrolled in any school, period, and African American children were far less likely to access schooling than their white peers. High schools only started to become common in the U.S. in the 1910s, and as late as 1940, less than half of Americans continued their formal education past the eighth grade. Different states instituted mandatory schooling at different times, and not until the 1950s were most American adolescents attending high school. Soon after that, school integration became a focus of the civil rights movement, and by the early '70s, almost all Americans attended high school and around 80 percent of high schoolers were graduating.

Yet despite all the changes schooling underwent in the real world, many teen books about school in the 1980s are, surprisingly, strikingly similar to books about school from a hundred years earlier. In Elizabeth Williams Champney's 1883 book *Three Vassar Girls Abroad*, which is widely considered to be the first school series for girls, the titular young ladies ran around having low-stakes, upper-middle-class, nonacademic adventures like old-timey Jessica and Elizabeth Wakefields (or, as the subtitle puts it, take "a vacation trip through France and Spain for amusement and instruction. With their haps and mishaps." Haps!). The same goes for subsequent books like Margaret Warde's *Betty Wales, Freshman* (1904), and *Grace Harlowe's Plebe Year at High School* and *The Merry Doings of the Oakdale Freshmen Girls*, both by Jessie Flower and both published in 1910. As the '80s and '90s school series novels in the following chapter show, even after the social battles of the '60s and '70s, a wide swath of school-novel protagonists continued to engage in no deeper activities than some haps and mishaps.

Introduction to Academic Social Structures

YA books of the '70s were often skeptical of school administrators (see: Paula Danziger's 1974 book *The Cat Ate My Gymsuit*) or of entire schools (see: Robert Cormier's *The Chocolate War*). In the school stories of the '80s, the opposite was true: school administrators just wanted what was best for students, and even if crappy stuff happened to them at school, it wasn't really the school's fault. School was essentially fun.

Case in point: Kate Kenyon's Junior High series, published from 1986 to 1988, which reimagined the most emotionally hideous

Nora has a stupid question.

HOW DUMB CAN YOU GET?

Kate Kenyon

Everyone in the eighth grade is leaving home!

THE GREAT EIGHTH GRADE SWITCH

Kate Kenyon

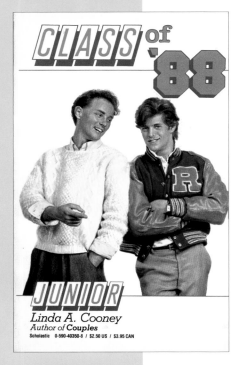

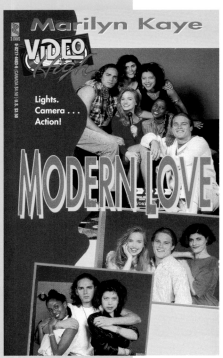

years of life as actually just kinda fun and silly. A typical Junior High heroine gave nerds makeovers, ran the school for the day, and traded families for the week, all while wearing "frilly white blouses that played up her peaches and cream complexion" and "trim khaki pants [that] showed off her trim figure." Their problems ran similarly light; in book #4, *How Dumb Can You Get?*, heroine Nora claims to have experienced "one of the worst mornings of my life" because some kind of motorized egg beater she constructed for shop class broke down. My junior high experience involved mean girls telling me that I "smell like hot butt," but you're right, Nora, not being perfect in shop class is also a problem.

But such airiness may have been the point. Rather than tuning out the experiences of those of us who spent eighth grade weeping in a bathroom stall, Junior High might have been trying to help its readers—who, like almost all YA and middle grade readers, were younger than the protagonists in the books they read—feel less scared about making the jump to junior high.

Other school-focused series had more of a structural gimmick, like Linda A. Cooney's Class of '88 and Class of '89 series. Each of these miniseries focused on a group of friends in a different high school class, and each book was named after a school year: *Freshman*, *Sophomore*, and so on. Though their title years and covers peg the books to a specific place and time (God bless that lemon-yellow sweater and button-down combo), the content is concerned with timeless issues like finding one's place in life and one's social circle, occasionally spiced up by mentions of '80s-specific trappings like Rubik's cubes or menacing punk rockers.

Yet other school series zoomed in, as it were, on a particular school pursuit, such as Marilyn Kaye's Video High series, which ran for nine books from 1994 to 1995 and follows the chaos that ensues when students at the school's TV channel are allowed to cover whatever their little *90201*-addled-hearts desire, such as teen sex surveys, drugs, and more. In its quest to rebrand AV activities as hip and not at all geeky, Video High yields more questions than answers, such as, why are these teachers giving the kids free rein on making programming? Are they worried about Sweeps Week? Isn't school TV supposed to cover forecasts and track-meet results? More to the point: who'd watch reports on drugs and sex surveys produced by a bunch of 17-year-olds? Wouldn't everyone at school rather go home and watch professional programming instead of hysterical lo-fi messes created by people with vendettas against the prom queen?

The students in '80s and '90s school series were usually upper-middle-class WASP-y kids having mostly WASP-y problems at a public school. But some exceptions existed, like Leah Klein's early 1990s series, the B.Y. Times. The protagonists are a group of girls who work on the school paper at an Orthodox Jewish school for girls ("B.Y." stands for Bais Yaakov), and the series, which ran for at least eighteen volumes, became so successful as to have a spin-off series (the B.Y. Times Kid Sisters). There's almost no record of the main series' existence today, besides a 2015 tribute by writer (and former child actor) Mara Wilson on the now-defunct blog *The Toast* and some pricey copies available on eBay.

In some ways, the B.Y. Times can be seen as just another part

Created and written by
LEAH KLEIN

The B.Y. Times ③

When it's twin against twin, there's bound to be trouble!

Twins in Trouble

Unlike their secular peers, the girls of the B.Y. Times cover illustrations wore clothes that were less '80s wacky and more classic and modest, reflecting their Orthodox faith.

of the parallel universe of religious pop culture knock-offs, like *Veggie Tales* or clean copies of *Die Hard,* in which Bruce Willis shouts "Yippee-ki-yay, Mr. Falcon!" But these books also point to the power of the formats and archetypes of girls' series, combining classic '80s problems about friendship stresses and school trouble with uniquely Orthodox Jewish predicaments like figuring out whether talking about others behind their backs is banned by the Torah or accidentally getting stuck in the middle of the Gulf War while visiting family in Israel(!!). But even though the group was in many ways the anti-BSC—as Wilson notes, "None of [the B.Y. Times heroines] ever talked about what they wanted to be when they grow up, other than mothers. All women were happy to have children and keep Shabbos. No one questioned authority."—those archetypes carried enough weight to cross cultures.

Go Directly to Detention, Do Not Pass Go

The era of kinder, gentler school lit didn't mean that problems never went down within the walls of your local junior high. It just meant that they were, on the whole, dealt with in moderate ways, even when the problems themselves were kind of harsh.

Schools were ground zero in the book-banning wars of the early '80s. Complaints made to the American Library Association about local communities prohibiting specific titles skyrocketed from 300 a year in the late '70s to more than 1,000 a year in 1981. These literary cultural wars are the grist for Betty Miles's 1980 coming-of-age novel *Maudie and Me and the Dirty Book*, in which Kate, an anxious 11-year-old conformist, learns the value of standing up for herself and her beliefs with an assist from classmate Maudie, a messy, spirited, emotionally vulnerable nonconformist. Yet it is Kate who ends up picking a so-called "dirty book" to read to a class of first-graders. (It's a picture book about the birth of a puppy! Fetch my smelling salts!) This, of course, provokes the younger kids' curiosity about where babies come from, which leads to small-town outrage and prompts a group called Parents United for Decency

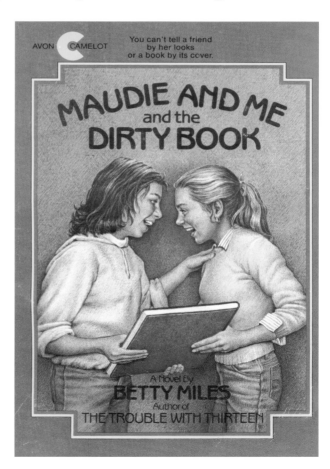

that wants to "keep filthy reading materials" away from kids to smear Kate as some kind of slatternly tween smut peddler. In timeless kid-lit fashion, Katie ultimately learns to be to herself and to ditch her Esprit-zombie pals in favor of the true-blue Maudie; but the book's examination of the consequences of censorship make it unusually meta and more subversive than other books of the genre. (Whether or not *Maudie* was ever banned because of its unflattering portrayal of overzealous pearl-clutching parents has been lost to the ages.)

Unlike Kate, the heroine of Barthe DeClements's 1985 book *Sixth Grade Can Really Kill You*, known as Bad Helen, is not an anxious conformist. She's pretty much the Bart Simpson of her school, always ready to prank a teacher with a homemade trip wire or vent her frustrations via swift application of spray paint

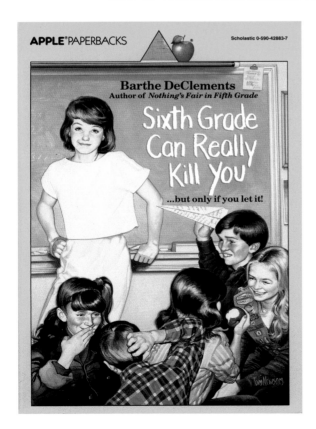

to school property. But Helen is no rebel sans cause; she acts out to deal with the stress of living with a learning disability, which her mother can't quite admit is real. When this book was published, the ink had barely dried on legislation supporting public-school kids with learning disabilities (a term that had been coined only in 1963), so the sympathetic portrayal of Helen's experience was relatively groundbreaking, although some parts feel thankfully outdated to the modern reader (including, I hope, the slur Helen's classmates hurl at her). But Helen's frustration, her mother's reluctance

A Kirkus review of *Our Sixth Grade Sugar Babies* gave a particular shout-out to its "engaging title and jacket" and called the book "thoughtful, well-crafted, and sure to be popular."

to acknowledge the disability, and the life-changing support of Helen's teacher still feel all too relevant.

What feels even more dated is the anti-pregnancy curricula that required kids to carry a sack of sugar, flour, or other baking ingredient around for the weekend in order to learn about the responsibility of caring for an infant. (Seriously. The *Philadelphia Inquirer* reported on schools using "egg babies" as early as 1986.) Vicki, the heroine of Eve Bunting's 1992 book *Our Sixth Grade Sugar Babies*, loses her sugar sack when she's busy checking out a cute boy, which may reveal the flaws inherent in the project: Is it really so easy to misplace a human baby, or to go to the grocery store and get a new baby? And do babies attract this many ants? These logical shortcomings are perhaps why the "raise a literal food baby" storyline is now only known as the one kind of sitcom plot less plausible than the "if we *have* to share a bedroom, we're going to split it down the middle with a painted line" plot.

Life Skills 101

Most novels set at school dealt with problems that were fairly trivial—forgotten lunch money, pop quizzes, the latest gossip about who's been banned for life from Pretzel Time. And that's great; can you imagine how much harder childhood would have been if every night you had to complete your social studies reading *and* absorb a nuanced lesson about the folly of man? But some school novels, just like some schools themselves, did occasionally engage with big issues.

Although real-life class presidents usually clinched victory simply by promising the senior class a trip to Six Flags, in Lael Littke's 1984 novel *Trish for President* every school government campaign has a manager who runs around yelling about strategy like James Carville commanding his war room, even though their strategy is rarely more complex than something you could've thought up on the bus ride to school. But *Trish* isn't really about bloodthirsty high school elections; it's about women in a small town at the dawn of the '80s trying to figure out what to do with the vestiges of second-wave feminism. Trish is running for president because alleged mega-hunk Jordan is also running, and it initially seems like a good way to get his attention. But along the way to Election

Day, Trish ponders whether "pushy" women are considered desirable by men, whether her homemaker mother is filled with regret about her career path not taken, and whether much has changed since her mom's day, anyway. She muses: "One part of me wanted to get out and prove to … everybody else that I could face the world and fight those barracudas. Another part just wanted to cook dinner for Jordan every night."

Trish never resolves her conundrum, which makes perfect sense. Littke's book was published in 1984, the same year presidential candidate Walter Mondale picked Geraldine Ferraro as his running mate, making her the first woman on a major party ticket, and as the relative controversy of their pairing demonstrated, pretty much no one at that time could agree on how women fit in to politics. (Thank God we've got that one figured out now, right, guys? Guys?)

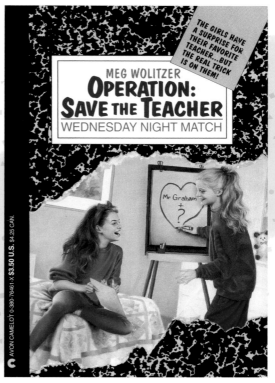

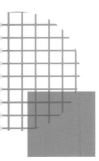

If few multi-book series dipped into big issues, fewer still organized themselves entirely around a single big issue. Operation: Save the Teacher from 1993 may be the only tween series ever to flow from the premise that a group of kids want to help a teacher who has just become widowed because his wife died in a car accident. Still, there's something far more remarkable about Operation: Save the Teacher, namely that it was written by Meg Wolitzer, author of *The Interestings* and other award-winning books that do not have soft-focus oil paintings on their covers. Regardless, the good intentions of the Save the Teacher schoolkids are somewhat overshadowed, at least for a modern adult reader, by the utter bizarreness of their pursuit. Stop trying to save that teacher! Just let him drink in peace, kids.

A more sophisticated take on teens, school, and death can be found in Janet Quin-Harkin's 1991 series Senior Year. As we learn from the cover of book #1: *Homecoming Dance*, "Kyle was gorgeous. Kyle was funny. Kyle was wild." We soon learn that Kyle is also dead, the casualty of a tragic drunk driving accident. While he was alive, he formed close emotional relationships with four girls from different cliques, who now happen to all be on the same school dance decorating committee cum grief support group ("I guess Kyle was really good at hiding his real self from people," one of them remarks, in what had started as a discussion of the dance's "undersea fantasy" theme). This connection is the core of the four-book miniseries; each volume flashes back to Kyle and his relationship with a specific girl, revealing more about her life as well as Kyle's unwitting march to doom. For example, in this first volume, we learn both that Joanie's exciting summer makeover made her more popular while straining her relationship with her best friend Brooke, and that Kyle thinks that driving after having four beers is no big deal. Senior Year feels less of a piece with other YA series than like an update of the Shangri-Las' "Leader of the Pack" for the *90210* generation. The shadow of Kyle's impending death lends gravitas to classic YA concerns like getting on prom court and figuring out whether or not a specific hunk is "out of your league," while also pointing out classic YA concerns are pretty low stakes compared to, you know, death.

Speaking of the unexpectedly grim: if you think, based on the title, that Jenny Davis's 1988 book *Sex Education* is a goofy teen sex romp, you would get an F. Narrator Olivia quickly and very frankly corrects that misconception in the beginning, stating, "I am sixteen years old. I am writing this at my desk in my room on the ninth floor of the University Psychiatric Hospital." In flashback, we see Olivia become friends with David after they are partnered up in an unorthodox ninth-grade sex-ed class. Assigned to "care for" someone, they pick Maggie, a fragile young pregnant woman who recently moved to the neighborhood with her husband. Olivia and David proceed to fall in (ninth-grade) love; Olivia explains, "Mrs. Fulton once asked our class did we think holding hands was a sexual act. A lot of kids sneered, but I knew better. I knew the answer to that one. It could be. It depended on who you held hands with, and how." But this

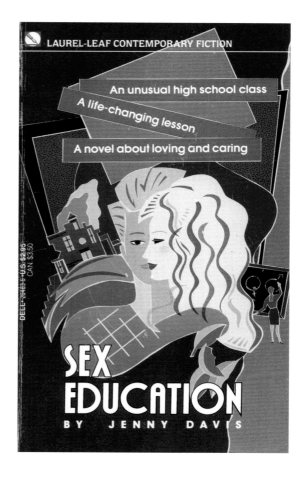

LAUREL-LEAF CONTEMPORARY FICTION

An unusual high school class

A life-changing lesson

A novel about loving and caring

DELL-20463-6 U.S. $2.95
CAN $3.50

SEX
EDUCATION
BY JENNY DAVIS

This cover for *Sex Education* is unusually abstract for a mass-market '80s YA novel—rare was the illustration that didn't portray the characters in a photorealistic style—and the taglines leave no doubt as to its gravitas (get your lessons! Get your loving and caring!), stressing more the "education" than the "sex" part.

warm fuzziness is short-lived. It turns out that Maggie is troubled because her husband is physically abusing her, and when David and Olivia try to get Maggie and her new baby to safety, Maggie's husband pushes David down the front stairs, killing him instantly. Olivia becomes catatonically depressed for six months, Maggie refuses to testify against her husband, and he's out of jail before a year is up. It's infinitely bleaker than *Meatballs*—and way better.

But how exactly does one package such an infinitely bleak YA novel? In this case, the answer is multiple covers, although neither proved particularly effective at representing the book's content. The book's original cover (see page 129) looks kind of like the logo for the Good Vibrations sex toy company, or possibly a body lotion from the '80s; a later cover (at left), designed to look like a school

binder, features a classic illustration of two kids at a desk. Neither approach quite manages to both stay true to the book and appeal to the post-BSC sophisticate; from a marketing perspective, it seems as though the publisher couldn't decide whether to shelve this title in the now-retro problem novel territory or lean on the titillating title and gloss it up to look like its contemporaries, the actual story notwithstanding. This identity crisis might be why this great, albeit dark, book seems to have been undeservedly lost down the teen fiction memory hole.

Extremely Advanced Economics

The '80s YA fascination with wealth seeped into school lit, producing a boomlet of books set in boarding schools—like regular schools, except for rich people! Unlike more classic boarding school novels like *The Catcher in the Rye* and *A Separate Peace,* these books weren't about unsupervised teens fumbling their way towards adulthood and occasionally pushing each other out of trees—in fact, the most famous boarding school series, the Girls of Canby Hall, is right at home with its BFF-driven contemporaries. The 33-book series, which debuted in 1984 and was written by the pseudonymous Emily Chase, tells the story of three roommates at a fancy-schmancy New England boarding school as they weather the hijinks, boy problems, and occasional kidnappings of your typical '80s YA series. Shelley, Faith, and Dana, the original Canby girls (they were replaced mid-series by a new class of students), were brainier than the average Wildfire heroine and more down-to-earth than any Wakefield, but their adventures generally failed to defy girls' series convention.

Still, in an era when YA bookshelves were a field of white faces, one of the series' primary heroines, Faith, was an African American girl (a full two years before Claudia Kishi would emerge on the scene). Moreover, the books immediately engage with the racial tension that Faith encounters at a predominantly white school. After white farm girl Shelley makes an ignorantly racist remark, Faith is rightfully pissed off, but, as writer and critic Mindy Hung has argued, the conflict is not handled particularly sensitively; the racist particulars are buffed out when all three roommates end up feuding over the remark. Missteps aside, having a heroine of color discuss racism in a light series YA novel was still a big deal—especially because Faith didn't exist solely to teach everyone about the realities of racism. She's a regular, silly teenage girl who befriends both of her roommates and ends up helping Dana

THE GIRLS OF CANBY HALL®

There are three new roommates in Room 407.

MAKING FRIENDS

EMILY CHASE

📖 Scholastic 0-590-40327-3 / $2.25 US / $2.95 CAN

prank her ex-boyfriend by the end of the first book. She was a full YA character—and that fullness included her experience of life in a racist society.

Of course, not all boarding school series were so thoughtful. Sharon Dennis Wyeth's Pen Pals series, which ran for 20 volumes from 1989 to 1991, focused on a foursome of schoolmates—Amy, Palmer, Lisa, and Shannon—who spend a lot of time writing to their male pen pals, while occasionally making time for other pursuits, like listening to Joan Jett or bragging about eating lobster. This was a rather paper-thin premise, but after the Great Middle Grade and YA Club-splosion, what clubs were even left? We could have very easily ended up with a series about a whittling society or (God forbid) Model U.N. In this case, the boarding school was just another layer of clubbiness that attempted to distinguish the series from its zillions of competitors.

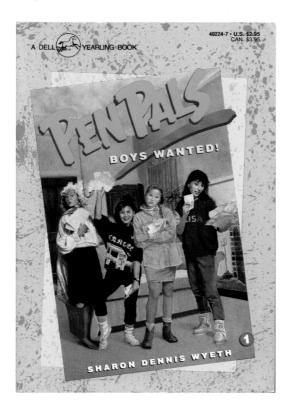

The cover of Pen Pals #1 makes no visual reference to its boarding school setting and instead leans heavily on the letter-writing angle (and funky outfits).

YA: The College Years

Like any precocious teen, the YA series was eager to enter the "real world" of college. Yet YA protagonists were hardly more mature than the average high schooler; a campus setting merely implied that there would be more "adult" stuff (aka sex and maybe drinking) side-by-side with the infantile tantrums and short-sighted thinking that made these series such delights to begin with. For example, Joanna Wharton's Campus Fever series, which ran from 1985 to 1986, didn't cover existential depression or student-loan horrors. Instead, the eight books introduced themes like sex and attempted suicide to the standard '80s YA series. And when the Wakefield twins made an exodus from Ned and Alice's house to

Sweet Valley University in 1993, little changed except that characters were suddenly able to guzzle booze to deal with their endless self-created personal problems. (Also, Jessica and Lila get married briefly to random dudes, but they both would have absolutely done so in high school had they been able, so it barely counts.)

In addition to awkward sex scenes, college YA also promised more problems per square inch, not least because the characters' parents aren't there to save them. This was the premise of Dahlia Kosinski's Reality 101 series; one cover's tag line read, "No parents. No rules. No turning back." (That cover also nixed '80s gauzy pastel paintings in favor of *90210*-evoking photos that seem to scream, "There will be sexual relations in this book!") The series, which lasted only two volumes published in 1995 and 1996, chronicled the lives of six sexy coeds sharing a house in Boulder, Colorado, that, judging from the cover, was located inside a Sprite ad. Characters hook up with one roommate after telling another roommate that they never hook up with roommates, or crash their car be-

cause they started drinking at 7 a.m., or make out with their gross-sounding boss and then are forced to model nude in the figure-drawing class that his wife teaches. You know, college stuff!

None of these college novels accurately renders the experience of attending college, but that was hardly the point. Seeing as the readers were nervous middle- and high-schoolers, these series were a soothing(ish) promise that college is less about leaving home for the unknown and more about reliving high school, except now you can have boys in your room! (Which of course is a lie, but so is most of what you learn in high school.)

CHAPTER 5

Jobs

BABYSITTERS, CAMP COUNSELORS, and TEEN SLEUTHS

Scholastic
0-590-43388-1 / $2.95 US / $3.95 CAN

#1

THE BABY SITTERS Club™

Four friends and baby-sitting—
what could be more fun?

Kristy's Great Idea

Ann M. Martin

In the past one hundred years, essentially everything about first jobs in America has changed. Historically, kids worked: in rural areas, they worked on family farms as soon as they were big enough to shovel horse poo, whereas city kids took dangerous jobs working long hours in factories. (Well, poor kids did, anyway; wealthy children were allowed to take it easy until they were made head of a bank or something.) But in the first half of the twentieth century, radical reformers convinced Americans that, hey, maybe these 9-year-olds should be in school instead of spending all day at the Asbestos and Flaming Knives Factory. And so, in 1938, with the passage of the Fair Labor Standards Act, 16 became the legal minimum age for most types of work conducted during regular school hours. Instead of toiling through double shifts, kids were now limited to working for shorter periods, in jobs that were less about bringing home the bacon than they were about trying on adult responsibilities, gaining maturity, and meeting other young people with whom to hump. Combine these changes in labor standards with a postwar economic boom, and by 1948, almost half of American teenagers were making their entry into the work force with a new thing called a summer job.

Around this time, girls' books fell hard for career girls, and every few years a new working character made her debut, like crime-solving news reporter Penny Parker (1939), crime-solving nurse Cherry Ames (1943), crime-solving flight attendant Vicky

Barr (1947), crime-solving model cum advertising exec Connie Blair (1948), and Sue Barton, a nurse who (tragically) solved no crimes at all (1936). These books made work seem like a glamorous, fun, and patriotic pursuit, rather than a necessary means of getting the money that keeps us from dying. In literature as well as in life, the lens had shifted.

Many of these career series ran until the mid to late '60s, when they, along with malt shop romances, were replaced in the hands and hearts of teen readers by realist fiction. Realist teens had jobs, sure, but their employment situations were rarely the driving force of a book's plot, conceit, or identity. But when the '80s rolled around, a lot of '40s and '50s YA trends were revived, among them books about jobs.

By and large, the protagonists of '80s kids career novels didn't *need* to work. These characters were upper-middle-class kids who sought out jobs for fun and notional profit. Considering that 20 percent of American kids lived below the poverty line in 1989, surprisingly few books included characters who worked because their families needed the money. Instead, they put forth a rosy capitalist vision of fulfillment and self-expression. In these books, work is about the pleasure of discovering yourself and enjoying new experiences—and if you can find someone who wants to pay you $3 an hour while you do it, all the better.

Even More Adventures in Babysitting

Once upon a time, babysitters did not exist. And it wasn't even that long ago. Before the babysitting movement of the 1920s, wealthy families hired full-time nannies to mind their brood, and if you weren't rich, you either watched your kids yourself or left them alone and hoped they didn't eat too many rusty tacks while you were away.

Similarly, there also was once a time when the Baby-Sitters Club did not exist: no Kristy's Krushers, no Kid Kits, no human being who would utter the sentence, "Today, for instance, I'm wearing purple pants that stop just below my knees and are held up with suspenders, white tights with clocks on them, a purple-plaid shirt with a matching hat, my high-top sneakers, and lobster earrings."

Basically, we lived in a world of darkness. But in the mid-1980s, Scholastic editor Jean Feiwel changed everything.

Earlier teen books had featured babysitters, of course, like Francine Pascal's novel *My First Love and Other Disasters* in 1979, Martha Tolles's 1985 book *Katie's Baby-Sitting Job*, and Willo Davis Roberts's 1985 novel *Baby-Sitting Is a Dangerous Job*. There were even nonfiction guides to the biz, like 1984 Scholastic Book Club selection *Baby-Sitting for Fun and Profit*. But Feiwel was the person who connected the dots. As the story goes, she had noticed that a book

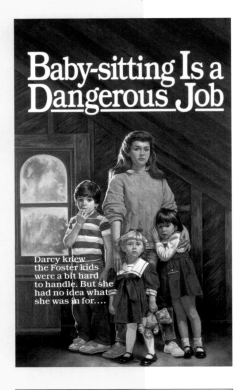

called *Ginny's Babysitting Job* was selling in school book clubs, despite getting almost no promotion. (In fact, no clear record of a book called *Ginny's Babysitting Job* exists. There is a 1963 book titled *Ginnie's Baby-Sitting Business* and *Katie's Babysitting Job* had been published in 1985, so it's possible that Feiwel conflated these two titles in interviews.) If one book about babysitters was working this well, four books about babysitting would be four times as good, right? So Feiwel approached Ann M. Martin, a former children's book editor who had published a few novels of her own, and asked her to come up with a miniseries about a group of babysitters, each with a unique trait or problem, who form a club. Thus, we had our babysitters:

Kristy Thomas: driven, tough, has a frighteningly intuitive understanding of capitalism

Claudia Kishi: creative, smart yet troubled at school, knows where to buy belts made out of feathers or short, baggy lavender plaid overalls

Stacey McGill: from New York, boy crazy, used to live in New York, dealing with diabetes, have you ever been to New York I used to live there it is extremely sophisticated

Mary Anne Spier: organized, shy, has a weird strict dad that kind of forced her to dress like a sister-wife

With her characters' traits assigned, Martin developed her own plot, and in 1986, *Kristy's Great Idea*, the first Baby-Sitters Club novel, was published. Originally only four books were planned, one told from each character's point of view, but the popularity of each volume made Scholastic sign up for more, and more, which led to the development of more characters with more traits:

Dawn Schafer: from California, environmentalist, Baby-Sitter most likely to not only have gone to Burning Man but to claim that she has a "playa name"

Jessi Ramsey: best friends with Mallory, good with languages, somehow an 11-year-old semi-pro ballerina

Mallory Pike: best friends with Jessi, has a ton of siblings, character about whom Martin once said she had no "strong feelings" regarding her post-BSC existence (seriously, check her 2010 interview with writer Catherine Garcia in *Entertainment Weekly*)

Abby Stevenson: Who? (For those of you who genuinely have no idea who this character is, Abby was the Janey-come-lately who replaced Dawn after she returned to California in the mid-'90s.)

Eventually, around 250 Baby-Sitters Club–related titles would be published, each tracking the characters doing way more than just hanging around Claudia's bedroom. Over the course of those books, the sitters created personals columns in the school paper (#71: *Claudia and the Perfect Boy*), deployed child psychology (#27: *Jessi and the Superbrat*), met dudes (#42: *Mary Anne and Too Many Boys*), waged class war (#11: *Kristy and the Snobs*), grappled with

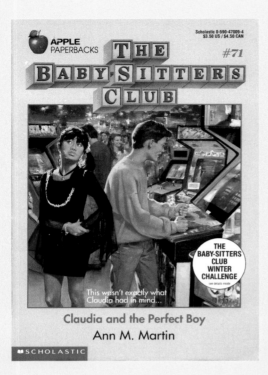

Scholastic 0-590-47009-4
$3.50 US / $4.50 CAN

THE BABY-SITTERS CLUB

#71

THE BABY-SITTERS CLUB WINTER CHALLENGE
see details inside

This wasn't exactly what Claudia had in mind...

Claudia and the Perfect Boy
Ann M. Martin

SCHOLASTIC

Scholastic 0-590-42502-1
$2.95 US / $3.95 CAN

THE BABY-SITTERS CLUB

#27

There's trouble for everyone when a TV star comes to town!

Jessi and the Superbrat
Ann M. Martin

SCHOLASTIC

Besides the consistency of format—square frame, alphabet-block letters—every Baby-Sitters Club title featured the name of the featured sitter, so it was easy enough to pick out the volumes about your faves (and check them off on the book order form). To the chagrin of copy editors and Merriam-Webster devotees everywhere, the series styles "Baby-Sitters" with a hyphen, mid-word capital S, and no possessive apostrophe.

Scholastic 0-590-43513-2
$3.25 US / $3.95 CAN

THE BABY-SITTERS CLUB

#2

Claudia's not sure she wants to find out who's on the other end of the line.

Claudia and the
Phantom Phone Calls
Ann M. Martin

Scholastic 0-590-42494-7
$2.95 US / $3.95 CAN

#34

THE BABY-SITTERS CLUB

Two weeks of sun, fun—
and boys galore!

Mary Anne and Too Many Boys
Ann M. Martin

Scholastic 0-590-43660-0
$3.50 US / $4.25 CAN

#11

THE BABY-SITTERS CLUB

Nobody's going to tell Kristy what to do—
especially not the Snobs!

Kristy and the Snobs
Ann M. Martin

Scholastic 0-590-43980-6
$2.95 US / $3.95 CAN

#23

THE BABY-SITTERS CLUB

Dawn's a California girl!

Dawn on the Coast
Ann M. Martin

Scholastic 0-590-33952-4
$2.50 US / $3.50 CAN

#3

THE BABY-SITTERS CLUB

Stacey's different... and it's harder on her
than anyone knows.

The Truth About Stacey
Ann M. Martin

chronic health issues (#3: *The Truth about Stacey*) contemplated a bicoastal lifestyle (#23: *Dawn on the Coast*), and thought they were being stalked by thieves, but were actually being stalked by boys too nervous to ask them out (#2: *Claudia and the Phantom Phone Calls*—fun fact: a teeny-tiny baby Kirsten Dunst actually modeled for the cover!). As of 2016, 178 million copies of BSC books were in print.

Almost all of us can identify if we're a Kristy, Claudia, Mary Ann, Stacey, Dawn, Jessi, or Mallory, and almost all of us made at least one failed attempt to start a babysitters club in our youth (turns out no one actually wanted a 12-year-old babysitter, plus someone always ended up skimming funds to buy Choco Tacos). But in seriousness, the stories of Kristy and company subconsciously shaped how a generation of girls conceived of our careers *and* ourselves. In an era of ambition-free, endlessly wealthy teen protagonists, the Baby-Sitters weren't just girls waiting for neighbors to dial them up for a gig; they actively organized and sought out opportunities. BSC wasn't singularly responsible for the career ambitions of Millennial women, nor is the series without flaws—obviously, the characters had the privilege to follow their professional bliss because they all came from well-off families. But ultimately, the series offered a fun, positive way of thinking about careers that few readers were exposed to at home, teaching us that with friends and just one really, really great idea, girls could make something meaningful.

Babysitting success begets babysitting imitators, including series that tried to fuse the BSC concept with other trends. Cherie Bennett's Sunset Island might have been the most successful of these hybrids; the series lasted for 33 volumes published between 1991 and 1997 simply by daring to imagine what would happen if the Baby-Sitters were *also* the Wakefield twins? We find the answer on the made-up rich person vacation area of Sunset Island, Maine, where Emma (the rich one), Carrie (the nerdy one) and Sam (the boy-crazy one), dwell in a semi-eternal summer. The girls work as au pairs, chase dudes, and engage in *Saved by the Bell*–style hijinks, like starting a band that gets signed to the record label owned by the father of a girl who hates you, competing in a beauty pageant against some other girls who hate you, and flashing forward ten years into the future for one volume in the middle of the series' run when the well of plot ideas runs dry. Cherie Bennett was a grand master of '90s teen job novels. She covered teen interns on an exploitative and incredibly popular TV talk show in *Trash* in 1997 and teens who want to become doctors in *University Hospital* in 1999, among others, always leaving readers with the most important business lesson of all: work is a great place to meet boys!

However, none of these mash-ups was quite as thrilling as Susan Smith's 1989 novel *Samantha Slade: Monster Sitter*. Aspiring tween babysitter Samantha earns the princely sum of $6 an hour to watch her supernatural charges, including a werewolf, a telekinetic, and the world's widdlest mad scientist. Despite all this, her adventures are relatively low-key; Samantha gets accidentally turned into a frog for a while, then starts a band with a vampire, but no one gets torn limb from limb by a pack of blood-lusting were-babies. For the Goosebumps reader who wanted more babysitting, or the BSC reader who wanted more lycanthropy, the Samantha Slade series was just the ticket.

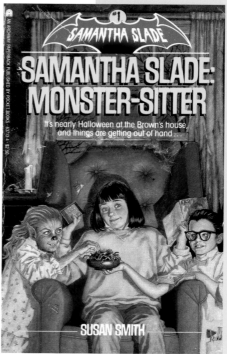

How a Cover Gets Made

When you think of the iconic Baby-Sitters Club covers, you're thinking of the artwork of a single person: Hodges Soileau. Though many series employed multiple cover artists, Soileau painted every single BSC cover except the first two, as well as the art for the BSC spin-off series, board games, calendars, and more.

To start, Soileau would get a written description from the publisher of what the cover was supposed to depict; he'd then create thumbnail sketches based on that description and book models for a photo shoot. A professional photographer took the photos, but Soileau supervised the shoots, sometimes helping solve visual problems, such as, in the example of an image for a BSC calendar, how to make the models look like they were on a rollercoaster (eventually, they arranged some chairs according to an old theme-park reference photo).

How does one land the plum gig of modeling for a BSC cover? Emi Soekawa, a former actress and model who posed for a number of YA book covers—including *Baby-Sitters Club Friends Forever Super Special: Graduation Day*, where she portrayed the divine Ms. Claudia Kishi (second from left)—was recruited from the modeling agency that represented her after high school. In Soekawa's experience,

models didn't get the chance to read the manuscript. When she'd arrive at the studio, the photographer or person managing the shoot "would come over and say 'Hey, in this book, the girls graduate from middle school,' or 'In this part of the series your boyfriend adopts a dog and you feel like he is weirdly obsessed with it,'" she said. "Then, if there were a series of photos, the photographer will usually give specific actions for each."

The modeling sessions provided memorable moments. On the cover of *Baby-Sitters Club #88: Farewell Dawn*, Dawn's mournful expression is not just about leaving the BSC—Soileau recalls that the model portraying her had suffered a concussion the previous day after falling off a horse! "She showed up for the shoot like a real trouper, and it worked out beautifully," he said. Soekawa recalled cover shoots "in a calm studio with a nice group of people," though they had occasional awkward moments, too. At the BSC shoot, Soekawa said, that at age 19, "I was clearly older than all the other girls. When we were leaving, one girl and I asked another if she wanted to go to Union Square and she told us she had to get back to [middle] school."

For photo covers, like the one Soekawa posed for, the shoot provided the final art. For painted covers, Soileau would then draw a graphite sketch. "The sketch would be approved by Scholastic (rarely were there changes)," Soileau told me in an email, "and, then I went to the finished painting," using oil paint on canvas or primed board.

But the biggest BSC-related question for any diehard fan is surely: *who picked Claudia's outfits?* According to Soileau, the publisher's description might have included details about clothing; when this happened, "I would talk this over with the photographer and when they booked the model, it was suggested that she bring something that might be close to the outfit described," he explained. "They also had extensive wardrobes at the photo studio! It never was a real problem as I recall!" There you have it—the mystery of Claudia's purple fedora finally solved.

"I think back and I'm very thankful, and feel very lucky to have had that opportunity," said Soileau. "I did something that was fun and also financially very rewarding . . . and the unbelievable opportunity to paint, paint, and paint some more has helped me be able to do what I do as a fine artist today."

For Soekawa, who now works in the publishing industry, being part of the BSC cover process was also personally meaningful. "When I was a little girl, I wrote a letter to Ann M. Martin asking if they ever needed a Japanese girl to pose as Claudia. There were really no other Asian, let alone Japanese, girls featured in series books and for this I will always be thankful to the series . . . [so] when I found out that I could maybe replace the girl that was Claudia on the covers, I was giddy."

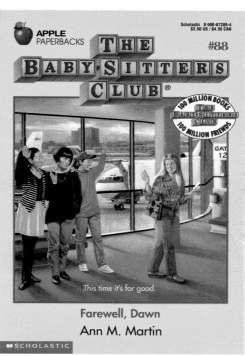

Farewell, Dawn
Ann M. Martin

It's a Dirty Job, But Some Tween's Gotta Do It

Though babysitting was the hot career ticket in the '80s and '90s, not everyone could hack it (plus the childcare market was absolutely flooded with overeager 12-year-olds). But jobs that took place outside a suburban rec room still had plenty to offer motivated teens. Coffee shops and restaurants were perennially popular places for the motivated teen worker who is also a motivated teen dater, providing the opportunity to find new love with your shift-mates as you sexily mop up some spilled barbecue sauce!

The basic structure of teen restaurant novels remained fairly consistent through the years: a teen needs to learn a life lesson, with a side order of love. In the Heartbreak Cafe series by Janet Quin-Harkin, which debuted in 1989, former rich girl Debbie isn't just trying to support herself when she locks down her first waitressing job; she's also proving her worth. But in addition to finding a sense of self-determination at the Heartbreak Cafe, Debbie also finds an adorable boy with whom she has exciting romantic tension. Eight years later, Elizabeth Craft's @Café series took the restaurant novel for a hard turn toward *My So-Called Life* territory, as the cover announces: "It's not the caffeine that's making everyone jumpy." Hmm, caffeine? As in, coffee? The beverage they serve in '90s countercultural mecca

Seattle?!? The titular @Café is San Francisco's coolest coffee shop, which happens to be staffed exclusively by sixteen-year-olds. Besides slinging lattes, the kids wear baby tees, go on internet dates with guys with usernames like Shyhunk, and run a website called *Spill the Beans* filled with info like horoscopes and tips on buying used cars, even though they're hardly qualified to offer either. As in many '90s career series, their professional duties don't impede these teens' ability to fall in secret love with each other, miscommunicate constantly, and, on occasion, find out that one of their mothers, whom they believed to be long dead, is in fact still alive.

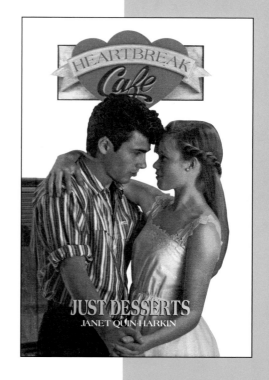

The hip barista gig was the dream. But most teens, like Lori, the heroine of Jana Ellis's Merivale Mall series, had to settle for a depressing food court gig. A twelve-volume series that debuted in 1988, Merivale Mall is a Sweet Valley High knockoff (down to the oval-inset illustration) set in a shopping center, focusing on mall worker Lori as she is repeatedly and bizarrely manipulated by her Lila Fowler–lite cousin, Danielle. Lori is supposed to be the down-to-earth one, but in fact she is as unrelatable as her rich evil cousin, like when she harshes on her parents' finances: "As a school principal and nurse, their salaries were

less than awesome." Yeah, Lori, how dare your parents have jobs focused on helping others! They should start selling junk bonds, like normal people! Despite—or maybe because of—the '80s cliché that is its setting, Merivale Mall had, and squandered, an opportunity to create a series that explores the specific dynamics of teen life in a mall. Imagine all the complications that ensue when a Contempo Casuals employee falls in love with someone who works at Benetton! Imagine the challenges faced by someone who literally needs their mall paycheck to survive! But such introspection was beside the point, and so we got another rich girl hellbent on crushing those around her.

On the complete opposite end of the gritty teen-employment spectrum from the civilized, air-conditioned confines of a shopping mall was the rarely featured job of . . . forest ranger. Kris Lowe's 1998 series Girls R.U.L.E. pair spirited BSC-type girls (The arty one! The sporty one! The one who used to live in New York!) with outdoor adventure as the gang becomes part of the first class of female junior rangers at their local national park. The group navigates national-park-type problems like rabid raccoons, poachers, forest fires, and pollution while also dealing with sexist adults and peers alike who say things like, "The last thing the rangers need is a bunch of girls running around the park getting in their way." Sadly, the outdoorsy girl market couldn't sustain a BSC level of success, and the series only lasted three books. But it was a solid effort to broaden the job market for fictional tweens, and I would like to believe that after the third volume, those girls made each and every one of those sexist boys eat a fistful of mulch.

Unlike the forest ranger, the camp counselor has a longer history in the world of young people's literature, though not an entirely happy one. In books like Glendon Swarthout's 1970 hit *Bless the Beasts and Children*, counselors were power-hungry jerks eager to abet any and all bullying in their decrepit and exploitative camps. But, as was true of many YA trends, these counselors softened in the

'80s, too, transforming from cruel oppressors to babysitters whose primary duties seem to be finding a make-out partner, fighting back against a mean girl counselor, and, if time permits, teaching some third graders to make a friendship bracelet or not drown in the creek or something.

As indicated by the ginormous type, this cover positions this Pascal book as, well . . . a Pascal book, not to be missed by any fans of Sweet Valley or Victoria (not to be confused with Caitlin—see page 33). A later rejacket would feature a photo of (then-unknown) actress Amanda Seyfried as the model.

Plotwise, these camps were often a kind of summer stage for mean girls to work up new material before the school year. Francine Pascal's *Love and Betrayal and Hold the Mayo!* from 1985 and Caroline Cooney's *Camp Girl-Meets-Boy* and its sequel, *Camp Reunion*, both published in 1988, all feature a nasty counselor who makes things hard for the rest of the staff. A sequel to *Hangin' Out with Cici*, Pascal's 1977 time-travel novel, *Love and Betrayal* follows heroine Victoria through her realistic, sadly time-warp-free summer of waiting tables at a summer camp. Victoria lusts after her

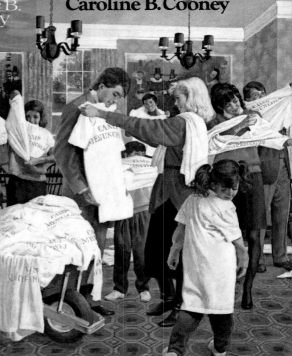

Fans of Caroline Cooney's *The Face on the Milk Carton* might not immediately recognize these camp-themed books as her work, thanks to their much more lighthearted covers. (Also, is that an indoor T-shirt wheelbarrow on the *Camp Reunion* cover? Is that even a thing?)

best friend's boyfriend, endures torture at the hands of mean girl Dena, and can barely pass even basic work proficiencies at her job. Meanwhile, Cooney's counselors—boy-crazy Violet and down-to-earth Marissa—toil at Camp Menunkechogue, aka "Camp Men," so named because it's a great place to find a date. Violet and Marissa work hard to make Camp Men live up to its name by checking out the local dudes, but eventually they join forces to fight back against the undermining counselor, Cathy.

The dirty business of convincing a bunch of children to obey you in the woods is addressed with a bit more in depth in Paula Danziger's 1980 book *There's a Bat in Bunk Five*. Marcy, the erstwhile heroine of *The Cat Ate My Gymsuit* from 1974, is now a counselor in training at an arts summer camp, where she is able to escape from her terrible family and, yes, have her first romance,

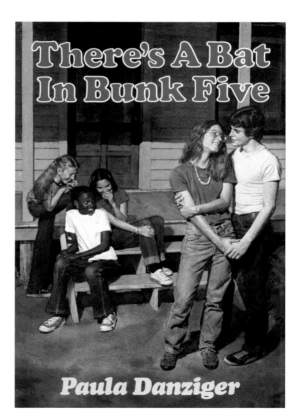

with a guy named Ted. But Marcy's summer is less about love than it is earning the respect of her campers, especially after her obsession with Ted leads her to miss warning signs from a troubled younger camper. Regardless, Marcy may be one of the best camp counselors in the genre, simply because she actually notices the campers.

Toward the YA end of the spectrum, covers made it clear that these weren't just books about lanyard-making and nature-walking, but about *love*. The giggling group of younger kids on the stairs further emphasizes that the time for childish things has passed, and k-i-s-s-i-n-g is where it's at this summer.

One job in '80s teen fiction is far grimmer than camp counselor, barista, or shopping mall sandwich artist. I speak, naturally, of the position of teen angel. In Cherie Bennett's Teen Angel series, which ran for six volumes in 1996, *angel* was not a metaphor: these girls were *dead*! (One of them overdosed on pills because she was upset about the SATs.) They reside in Teen Heaven, a netherworld limbo overseen by (I kid you not) James Dean, who makes them go to Teen Heaven High and take jobs on earth that will allow them to perform good deeds. This all unfolds in, like, the first five pages of book #2: *Love Never Dies*, making the rest of the series—the teen angels journey to earth to help other teens in mortal danger, one becomes a ski instructor and crushes out on a living guy—seem underwhelming

simply by comparison. Sure, it may sound preposterous, but does it make much less sense than having teens manage your cybercafé?

But what about the teens who were still alive, hated the outdoors, got fired from their gig at Spencer's Gifts for abusing the employee discount, *and* couldn't steam soy milk to save their life? The professional-teen series boom offered yet another option: doctor. For the teens of Diane Hoh's Med Center series,

As if teen angels weren't a far-out enough concept to wrap your earthly head around, *Love Never Dies* throws in the ski-instructor angle, which probably makes more sense on the page than it does on the cover (in fact, take away the cloud-riding girls in the background and this could pass for a novel about a young Lindsey Vonn).

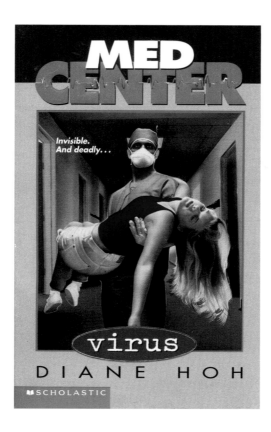

Despite TV medical dramas gaining fans thanks to sudsy interpersonal relationships, and no doubt buoying the teenage novel spin on the concept, the grim, shadowy artwork of *Med Center* pushes the "deadly infectious disease" angle harder than the "could be George Clooney under that mask" angle.

getting board certified before reaching the age of majority was a breeze, possibly because all the hospitals were woefully under-staffed thanks to constant disasters, both natural and man-made. In the first book, 1996's *Virus*, a deadly illness sweeps through the berg; in later volumes, the poor denizens of Grant, Massachusetts, suffer through flooding, blizzards, fires, and a crazed nurse who is trying to kill everyone. It was truly the Seattle Grace of its time! The premise of doctors having to rely on a group of blandly charm-ing, lightly horny teens to help them out because there are just not enough adult physicians to go around is about as plausible as teen angels, but hospitals have been a seat of soap operatic drama since time immemorial (and *E.R.* had breathed new life into the genre in 1994), so why not stretch credulity to capitalize on the trend?

What's a Nice Tween Like You Doing in a Place Like This?

Teen detectives enjoy a work life that offers a tantalizing combination of independence, agency, forcing adults to take you seriously, and almost getting killed. However, helping recover the Baroness's candelabra or freeing Old Man McGillicutty from the old mill was rarely a paying gig, so maybe these teen crime-busters are more like volunteers or unpaid interns. But compensation notwithstanding, mystery solving is one of the longest-running jobs for fictional kids. The Ruth Fielding series introduced the mystery genre to girls' series books in 1913; in 1930, Nancy Drew became an immediate

success, and in the following years sleuths like Judy Bolton, Beverly Gray, Kay Tracey, the Dana Girls, and Trixie Belden were introduced in efforts to capitalize on the trend.

Nancy, the OG girl detective, remained popular throughout the YA shake-ups of the '60s and '70s, although she didn't exactly engage with the times. In 1968, Harriet Adams, head of the Stratemeyer Syndicate, the book packager that created Nancy Drew, told *New York Times* reporter Judy Klemesrud that the books intentionally "don't have hippies in them. And none of the characters have love affairs or get pregnant or take dope. If they did, I'm sure that would be the end of the series." (Adams also had trouble understanding why people were upset about the racism in the original Nancy volumes, so go figure.)

But change seeped in after Adams's death in 1982. With the Nancy Drew Files series that debuted in 1986, Simon and Schuster created a new Nancy Drew for a new era. Our heroine engaged in new, '80s-appropriate activities like attending artisanal chocolate festivals, fighting great white sharks, and, as you can see from the cover of #58: *Hot Pursuit*, wearing Zubaz while standing in front of an exploding amplifier. The books also cranked up Nancy's once thoroughly G-rated romantic interests; this iteration of the girl detective dated around and had *intense* feelings about good ol' Ned Nickerson. She never chucked it all to investigate human rights abuses in the developing world or anything, but for a successful long-running mystery series, this reboot counted as a major overhaul.

No mystery series in the '80s and '90s took off to Nancy or even Trixie Belden levels of success, but several tried to do so, usually while brandishing a gimmick or two.

Mike and Ally Mysteries by Blossom Elfman (Danny Elfman's mom!)

DEBUTED IN: 1989

GIMMICK: Mike and Ally are different from each other. Really, really different. Ally is hot and popular, and Mike is a nerd. Also, Ally is in love with Mike, but Mike thinks Ally is a bimbo. Also, Ally says stuff like, "Mike knows a lot of academic stuff, but he doesn't know doodley about danger." Somehow, their contrasting traits help them solve small-town mysteries about murdered teachers and secret Cold War experiments.

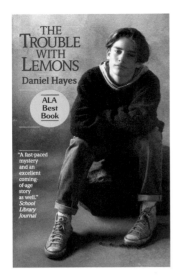

The Trouble with Lemons by Daniel Hayes

DEBUTED IN: 1991

GIMMICK: Displaced rich kid from L.A. Tyler and up-state New York townie Lymie bridge the Reagan-era class divide to solve small-town crimes. The first book's cover serves as a living document of the '90s teen heartthrob hairstyle trend known colloquially as the "butt cut."

Tripper and Sam by Nancy K. Robinson

DEBUTED IN: 1986

GIMMICK: This showbiz-adjacent series pairs hot daughter-of-a-documentarian Tripper with Sam, a teenager who is somehow also already a soundman on films. They solved mysteries about evil movie producers, jewel thieves, and the like. Typical. (I mean, as typical as being a professional teenage soundman!)

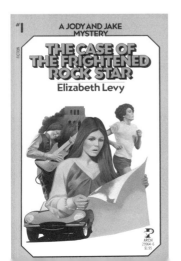

Jody and Jake Mysteries by Elizabeth Levy

DEBUTED IN: 1980

GIMMICK: Just like the Bobbsey Twins, Jody and Jake are sibling detectives. Unlike the Bobbsey Twins, they're teens and they have bitchin' late '70s/early '80s hair. They also share '80s-era Nancy Drew's penchant for standing in front of guys shredding on the guitar.

Crosswinds by various authors

DEBUTED IN: 1987

GIMMICK: Crosswinds was Harlequin's short-lived YA line whose titles ran the gamut from *Even Pretty Girls Cry at Night* to *Lou Dunlop, Private Eye*. I think these books were supposed to be romantic mysteries, but the cover of book #11, *Shock Effect* by Glen Ebisch, suggests otherwise. (Or maybe an image of a woman shrieking at a dead body read differently to audiences in 1987 than it does today.) Several authors contributed to the series, including a brash young iconoclast named R. L. Stine.

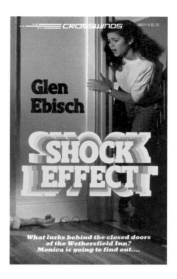

Spy Girls by Elizabeth Cage

DEBUTED IN: 1997

GIMMICK: The Spy Girls are what happens when you record an episode of *Charlie's Angels* over a VHS copy of *Clueless* while reading a Delia's catalog and chugging Mountain Dew till your eyes cross. Three international teen spies do things like infiltrate high-end wellness cults while saying things like "mondo browse fest" and making *Dilbert* jokes.

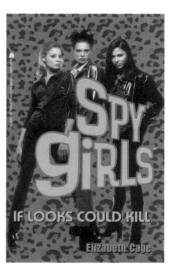

Though it's easy to rag on these books for ignoring the winds of change, sometimes you just want to read a romp about a dead body or a purloined tiara! But in an era when depictions of teens changed several times over, and the books about them at least attempted to touch on social change, it's worth noting that teen detectives often changed nothing but their hairdos.

I'm Gonna Be a Supermodel

If you couldn't get hired as a babysitter, a camp counselor, or an unpaid detective, '80s and '90s YA had one final opportunity for you: you could become a *star*! Career series like BSC were all about being down-to-earth, but the era's penchant for soap opera dramatics (fueled by the dueling prime-time-TV juggernauts *Dallas* and *Dynasty*, which debuted in 1978 and 1981, respectively) leaked into career novels, presenting young female readers with an ever-growing slate of books about jobs that we would never, ever, ever have.

Which is not to say that these jobs were *fun*. Nothing about All That Glitters, the fictional soap opera at the heart of the eponymous six-book series from 1987 and 1988, seems all that great (except for the giant sleeves on those ballgowns, which are pretty ace). Naive Katie befriends her worldly costar Shana, who comes from a prestigious acting family; she eventually steals Shana's boyfriend. This is hardly a good thing to do, but if you were a teen soap opera star in 1987, wouldn't you probably get into more dramatic stuff, like taking all four members of Mötley Crüe as your dates to the Daytime Emmys or throwing a fit in TCBY when they wouldn't comp you a cone of fat-free vanilla? I guess Katie and Shana are better people for keeping things chill, but that doesn't necessarily make them all that fun to read about. The high-stakes, soapy, *Dynasty*-esque vibes begin and end with the cover (which, ultimately, might be enough to get someone to buy it).

Even less dramatic is Alane Ferguson's 1993 novel *Stardust*, which, admittedly, is about a middle schooler, who probably

Their lives are a soap opera—on and off the screen! 8

ALL THAT GLITTERS

AWARD NIGHT

· A BANTAM BOOK ·

KRISTI ANDREWS

HOW DO YOU GO FROM BEING A
STAR TO JUST BEING YOURSELF?

ALANE FERGUSON

STARDUST

shouldn't be consorting with rock stars. Haley has been playing a Stephanie Tanner–type moppet called Samantha Love on a show called *Family Love* since she was 2 years old. When she is written off her show, the ex-starlet has to adjust to living as an average sixth grader in a small midwestern town, and the story is less "glam tales from a life you'll never have" and more "stuck up middle schooler gets called on her bullshit and becomes a better person." Still, it's easy to see how prime-time sitcom fans would flock to this virtual roman à clef about life beyond the camera lights.

One unexpected source for '90s YA showbiz drama was Isla Fisher. Before she was starring in movies like *Wedding Crashers* and *Bachelorette* and being mistaken for Amy Adams, Fisher

was a teen actress in her native Australia, where she starred in a soap opera called *Home and Away.* And like Britney Spears, Hilary Duff, and Nicole "Snooki" Polizzi after her, Isla decided that being a young TV celebrity should not prevent her from writing a YA novel. In fact, she wrote *two*, both with her mother, Elspeth Reid, and both published in 1995: *Seduced by Fame* and *Bewitched.* The novels are blessedly tawdry and ridiculously dramatic, and they thoroughly investigate the hazards of being an attractive teen with professional ambitions. In *Bewitched,* for example, hottie Valentina is a great dancer with an overbearing mother who travels to Russia to perform with the

Bolshoi Ballet, make out with a hot guy, look for her father, and then realize that the correct hot guy to make out with was the one who had been supporting her the whole time.

Classic soapy teen romance stuff, of course. But the thing that most sets *Bewitched* apart from its compatriots is the "Letter from Isla" at the book's end, which is published in a weird, Comic Sans–esque font evocative of handwriting to suggest how close you and Isla have become over the course of the book. In fact, you guys are now so close that Isla's become kind of emotionally needy: "Did you like it?" she demands to know. She then chattily admits that her mom did most of the writing because she was busy with her soap opera. She *then* promises a future novel about separated-at-birth twins, which doesn't seem to have ever been published, and goes on to note that ballet is "about as glamorous as working on a TV soap. Not!" Oh, to be 17. And on a TV soap. In 1997.

Bewitched stands in the shadow of the many YA books about semi-pro ballet dancers that came before it, including Karen Strickler Dean's Maggie Adams stories. Starting with *Maggie Adams, Dancer* in 1980, the series follows the trials and tribulations of Maggie as she goes from a 15-year-old dancer in training battling against obstacles like an unsupportive boyfriend and a dad who thinks she should study something more practical to, in 1986's *Stay on Your Toes, Maggie Adams*, being a 19-year-old apprentice prima ballerina battling against obstacles like . . . an unsupportive boyfriend. The same unsupportive boyfriend, in fact, who is not sympathetic to the reality that jobs as an apprentice prima ballerina are hard to come by. This is why Maggie won't leave San Francisco to go live with him in Boston—she can't find new work out there, to which Doug responds by throwing a fit and claiming, "You don't love me enough!" (Frickin' Doug! Aren't they all named Doug?) Like other showbiz books, YA books about life as a professional dancer were short on realism, but the Maggie Adams novels' depictions of stress caused by a boneheaded boyfriend are sadly rather true to life.

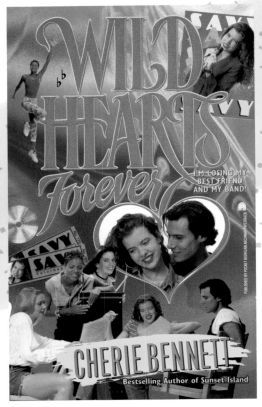

If you couldn't cut it as a professional teen actor *or* dancer, my condolences. But tweens and teens had yet another shot at fame in the pre-Napster years: rock star! Cherie Bennett, she of the many teen career series (see pages 146 and 156), dug into the world of all-girl teen country bands in Wild Hearts, starting with a cover that promises to give readers the inside scoop on essential teen-musician activities, from Jazzercise to sitting around idly holding drumsticks. Over the course of this six-book series, all published in 1994, surly New York teen Jane moves to Nashville, where she experiences nothing but nasty culture shock after nasty culture shock until she joins the pit band for the school musical. And naturally, like all school bands, the ensemble evolves into all-girl country band called the Wild Hearts, a group that becomes the perfect backdrop to examine hot teen issues like self-confidence, makeovers, and being rich but having a mean family. And all this four years before the Dixie Chicks made their major-label debut!

Not all books about glamorous careers extol them as great options for your average middle schooler; some zero in on how ludicrous it is for a regular tween to actually embark upon one. Though you may know Lois Lowry best from such emotionally hardcore middle grade fare as *Number the Stars* and *The Giver*, she also spent the '80s and half of the '90s exploring her lighter side in nine books about Anastasia Krupnik, an adorkably neurotic goofball tween who regularly communed with a bust of Sigmund Freud. This wacky adolescent intellectual's coming-of-age adventures skewed a little different from those of her peers: Anastasia catfished guys whose personal ads ran in the *New York Review of Books* and once accidentally got a job as a maid.

Book #7, 1987's *Anastasia's Chosen Career*, flirted with one of the most loaded teen glamour professions of the '80s: modeling. A class paper on her career plans has Anastasia plotting to take a modeling course; naturally, she lies to her professorial parents and says it's all part of a scheme to start a career as a bookstore owner. (Shelving Jane Austen novels and getting covered in vegetable oil and writhing around on the hood of a Jaguar—are they really so different?) Anastasia makes friends in modeling school, learns that maybe she would in fact prefer to be a bookstore owner, and, most

40100-3 • U.S. $3.50
CAN. $4.50

A DELL YEARLING BOOK

By the author of the Newbery Medal winner *Number the Stars*

LOIS LOWRY

ANASTASIA'S CHOSEN CAREER

Linda wanted the crown,
but Arlene would do...

ANYTHING
TO WIN!

GIRLS

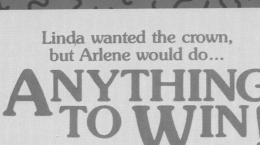

DREAM

1

CREATED BY
....
ROSEMARY
JOYCE

AN ARCHWAY PAPERBACK PUBLISHED BY POCKET BOOKS • 62110-6 • $2.50

important, keeps the harebrained schemes coming.

Interestingly, although Anastasia's tales are never about anything more hardcore than being the smart-alecky child of Jewish intellectuals, the Anastasia books were among the most challenged for younger readers in the '80s and '90s, according to the American Library Association. This is allegedly due to the fact that Anastasia drinks the foam off her dad's beer and knows about bra stuffing, aka has any fun in this god-awful world. (These details were sadly edited out of the recent reissue of the series, which tells you everything you need to know about the bleak times in which we live.)

After the Miss Teen USA competition flounced onto the stage in 1983, yet another backdrop for a drama-ridden YA series was born. Rosemary Joyce took on the cutthroat world of beauty pageants, where teen girls apparently use the phrase "nose candy" without a hint of irony, in the Dream Girls series, published from 1986 to 1987. Innocent Linda is naturally gorgeous and vivacious (no nose candy required for her, thank you!) and an instant success on the pageant circuit, while competitor Arlene sets traps (like ripping Linda's competition dress!) that Linda easily avoids (she, uh, wears a different dress). Arlene also tries to steal Linda's boyfriend, but later on, the two become friends and unite to deal with evil pageant queen August (she of the nose candy!). All of it adds up to six volumes full of boyfriend stealing, pageant sabotage, evil stage moms, and lines like, "But maybe you've forgotten that little incident last year when you stole Ted Blane's school files and then concocted that story that he was a drug addict when he was only taking pain killers." The job of beauty queen was barely work, but it could be a career—in the '80s, at least—and for a YA series, that was more than enough.

CHAPTER 6

Danger

TRAGEDY, TABOO TOPICS, *and* OTHER TOUGH STUFF

A BANTAM STARFIRE BOOK ★ IN U.S. $3.99 (IN CANADA $4.99) ★ A BANTAM BOOK ★ 28958-5

THE FACE
ON
THE MILK
CARTON

CAROLINE B. COONEY
author of *Operation: Homefront*

You may know them as problem novels, social novels, issue novels, or novels that you had to hide from your mom. Nomenclature aside, the objective of YA books about "taboo" issues like eating disorders, drug abuse, or sexual assault has remained constant: to make readers feel more informed and less alone. But the taboos themselves changed throughout the '80s and '90s, and so did the books.

Early problem novels dealt with a handful of topics, including abortion (Paul Zindel's *My Darling, My Hamburger* from 1969; see page 205), teen parenthood (Ann Head's *Mr. and Mrs. Bo Jo Jones* from 1967), and sexual assault (Richard Peck's *Are You Alone in the House?* from 1967). But in the '70s the category began to bloom, delivering a tidal wave of books about topics from drugs (*Go Ask Alice*; *Kathleen*; *A Hero Ain't Nothing but a Sandwich*; *The Late, Great Me*), to running away from home (*Go Ask Alice* again, *To Take a Dare*, *Steffie Can't Come Out to Play*, *See Davy Run*), to parental abuse (*Don't Hurt Laurie!*), to rape (*Did You Hear What Happened to Andrea?*) and what is understood today to be statutory rape (*Love Is One of the Choices*). By the end of the '70s, these books were basically synonymous with YA lit.

Teens in '80s issue novels, by contrast, dealt with external threats—kidnappers, random violence, sudden illness—or threats from inside themselves—depression, eating disorders, suicide. It was "not a tonal shift, but a real shift in genre and attitude," according to Cathryn Mercier, director of the Children's Literature Program at Simmons College. Teens in trouble weren't "juvenile delinquents" or "dropouts"; instead, they were considered "at risk" and offered counseling, housing, and other social services. (Of course, these new cultural attitudes applied largely to white, affluent teens while teens of color and poor teens were regularly demonized in the media and marginalized in YA.)

Meanwhile, parental anxiety was at an all-time high, thanks to high-profile kidnappings, shocking (and eventually debunked) sexual abuse allegations against various U.S. daycare centers, news reports on a (nonexistent) teen suicide epidemic, milk carton kids, and "stranger danger." No longer were children free to roam their neighborhoods freely, befriending rusted nails and eating wet cigarette butts at their leisure; they were sheltered, seat-belted, and never not in danger. The kids were all right; the world was the problem.

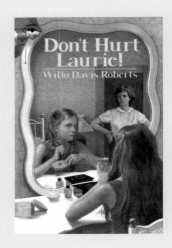

Snatched, Stalked, and Surveilled

The stranger danger terror of the '80s begat a juggernaut of a publishing trend: books about kidnappings. Largely absent from '70s YA, this topic was omnipresent in books of the '80s and '90s, with a varietal to match any mood or deeply repressed fear you could conjure up.

Some books featured kidnappings by the child's parent, such as Norma Fox Mazer's 1981 book *Taking Terri Mueller*. Terri thinks her mother died when she was a baby, but in reality, her father abducted her when her parents divorced; the heroine of Susan Beth Pfeffer's 1996 book *Twice Taken* finds herself in a similar situation. In Auline Bates's *Mother's Helper*, published in 1991, an au pair comes to realize she's working for a mother who kidnapped her own baby. And in Charlotte St. John's Red Hair series (see page 108), parental kidnapping and death-faking are used to dramatically split up twin sisters Elaine and Emily.

But kidnapping by nonparent strangers was far more sensational, and one such story became the gold standard of kidnapping books, still in print and popular almost thirty years after it was published: Caroline Cooney's 1990 novel *The Face on the Milk Carton* (see page 172). The moment when Janie Johnson sees her own childhood photo on a missing child alert on the side of a milk carton is indelibly imprinted on the memory of this generation of readers (seriously, bring it up at a party). Janie's sudden realization that there's more to her life than what her older, mysterious parents have told her is famous not just

> **For me, it was primarily a book about worry: parental worry. It was a book where I didn't want any bad guys. I wanted everyone in the story to be a good person trying to do the right thing when there isn't necessarily a right thing to do. Therefore, the kidnapper is off stage and not really of interest. It isn't her story.**
>
> —CAROLINE COONEY

Shadowy images of a beautiful, blonde white girl nervously pressing a phone to her ear are a horror staple—think Drew Barrymore's iconic turn in *Scream*. (Sadly, this cover layout doesn't seem to have accounted for indent created by the book's spine, leaving one of our heroine's eyes weirdly creased.)

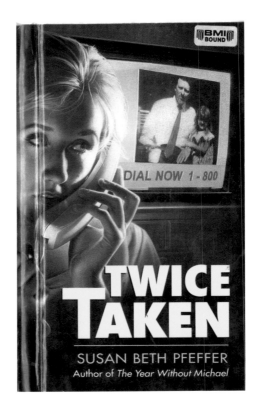

because it's such a unique and evocative instant of horror; it's also a moment that perfectly sums up this particular '80s zeitgeist. In Janie Johnson's milk carton moment—as well as her subsequent discovery that she was not the Johnsons' biological daughter, but in fact had been kidnapped from her birth family by the Johnsons' unstable biological daughter, Hannah—Cooney depicted on the page the dominant parental panic of the era, as well as helped untangle that fear for readers.

Janie's story continued for five books, the last of which, *Janie Face to Face*, was published in 2013. In that book, Janie ends up with her old boyfriend Reeve, and the kidnapper Hannah finally faces justice. More than bringing a sense of closure to the story, this conclusion doubles down on the series' message that even in the darkest situations, we can sometimes find hope.

To say that few other kidnapping books shared this optimistic point of view is an understatement. In fact, another of the era's best-known kidnapping novels, Ouida Sebestyen's 1989 book *The Girl in the Box*, is basically a Voltron made of the culture's grimmest beliefs about child abduction. All the essentials are there: a kidnapping that occurs while the child is innocently walking through the streets of her hometown; a hideous and insensible crime that pushes the limits of human understanding; an ambiguous ending that implies but never states the heroine is dead. No wonder so many of this book's GoodReads reviews are written by adult women who are still traumatized by having read this in middle school.

The titular girl living inside the so-called box, Jackie, is abducted off the street by a creepy man with a creepy van; he ties her up,

pulls a pillowcase over her head, and deposits her in a tiny, pitch-black, windowless room, where her only company is a box of stale pastries, a glass of gross water, and her typewriter (which she, extremely conveniently for the sake of the narrative, just happened to be carrying in her backpack). Her typewriter allows her to tell the stories that make up the book; in the dark, Jackie touch-types letters to the family and friends she may never see again, as well the authorities who she hopes will find her, and we read over her shoulder, not a little terrified. *The Girl in the Box* is primo tween nightmare fuel, not just because Jackie's captivity is grade-A torturous, but also because we never get to learn why

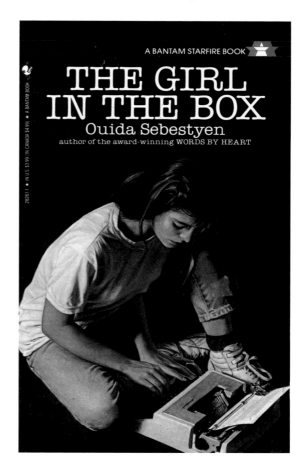

A BANTAM STARFIRE BOOK

THE GIRL
IN THE BOX
Ouida Sebestyen
author of the award-winning WORDS BY HEART

Jackie was kidnapped, or why her kidnapper left her alone to die. The story channeled the era's omnipresent fear of random, violent, spontaneous abduction in an unmarked van. If *Milk Carton* connected with our pervasive worry that parents can't perfectly protect their kids, *Girl* engaged with a much darker fear: that monsters walk among us everywhere, and there's nothing we can do to avoid them.

Another pervasive crime fear gripping the nation that showed up in '80s YA was stalking. This decade was when most Americans learned what stalkers were; one killed John Lennon in 1980, and another attempted to kill Ronald Reagan a year later (to "impress" the person he was stalking, Jodie Foster). Further headline-grabbing crimes, including the 1989 death of actress Rebecca Schaefer at the hands of her stalker, led to the first U.S. anti-stalking law, which was passed in California in 1990 (yup, until then, it was not expressly illegal to stalk someone).

A frank novel about the nightmare of rape and its aftermath.

Are You in the House Alone?
Richard Peck

"A Best Book of the Year"
– School Library Journal
"Recommended."
– ALA Best Books for Young Adults

The original teen novel about stalking, Richard Peck's *Are You Alone in the House?*, was published in 1976, a few years before stalking fever swept the nation, but it pioneered many of the genre's narrative beats—like the creepy, mysterious lead-up and the dangerous confrontation with the stalker—and resolves with a rather sensitive treatise on the problems that survivors of stalking and sexual assault encounter in society. As the hysteria increased toward

Desperate Pursuit

Gloria D. Miklowitz
author of *Suddenly Super Rich*

50095-5 ∗ IN U.S. $3.99/IN CANADA $4.99 ∗ A BANTAM BOOK

the end of the '80s, so did the number of stalker horror novels, like Carol Ellis's *My Secret Admirer* (see page 234), although many played off the stalking more as a thrilling, lurid mystery than an it-could-happen-to-you trauma. However, some stories, like Gloria D. Miklowitz's 1992 novel *Desperate Pursuit*, were more realistic and treated stalking like a violent crime instead of a titillating puzzle.

Miklowitz wrote more than sixty books in her career, some with titles like *Natalie Dunn: World Roller Skating Champion*, but most of which grappled forthrightly with social issues. In *Desperate Pursuit*, 15-year-old Nicole drops her extremely clingy boyfriend Michael to go out with the hunky and less-clingy Shane. But Michael isn't just a creepy boyfriend; he's also a creepy stalker, who mounts a campaign of harassment that culminates in his shooting at Nicole as she and Shane prepare to go to prom. (Shane is wounded, and Nicole talks Michael down until the police can nab him.) Though the plot points of *Desperate Pursuit* feel similar to the more lurid Point Horror stalking stories published by Scholastic, Miklowitz doesn't paint Michael as a *Friday the 13th*-esque unbeatable evil, as many horror stalkers were. Instead, stalking is portrayed as a violent crime, and Michael as not a monster, but a human offender who, Nicole hopes, will finally "get the psychological help he's needed for a long time." And yet, for all its pragmatism in crafting a relatively nonsensational stalking story, *Desperate Pursuit* couldn't escape a campy cover, complete with a blood-red title and a black rose sinisterly clasped behind the back of what looks like Bruce Springsteen's *Born in the U.S.A.* album cover.

Just Say "Whatever"

Drugs and the '80s are inextricably linked. This was the decade of D.A.R.E. and the "this is your brain on drugs" PSAs, of Melle Mel's song "White Lines" and Nancy Reagan's antidrug guest appearance on *Diff'rent Strokes*, of racist drug laws that penalized poor, primarily African American crack users but not wealthy, white yuppies who freely snorted coke until they thought Phil Collins sounded *amazing*. So it's surprising that this era of such pervasive antidrug paranoia didn't yield many enduring antidrug novels, which were a centerpiece of '70s YA. (You may recall 1971's hit *Go Ask Alice*, a book about a wholesome, nerdy teen who tries

drugs by accident at a party and becomes so debauched so quickly that she's basically selling heroin to members of Led Zeppelin by the next weekend.)

Among the few are *Connie*, published in 1982 by religious writer John Benton, about a girl with a negligent mom who becomes addicted to drugs and is on the road to nowhere until she is sent to a Christian home for girls (like the one Benton operated in real life). Similarly, H. B. Gilmour's 1986 novel *Ask Me If I Care* tells the story of alienated 14-year-old Jenny, who feels so lost and confused after her parents' divorce that she starts getting high to impress Pete, her hot, no-goodnik next-door neighbor. And a few books feature

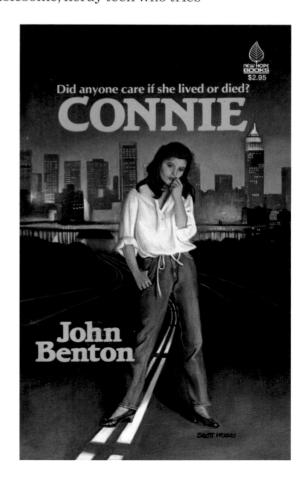

Did anyone care if she lived or died?
CONNIE
John Benton

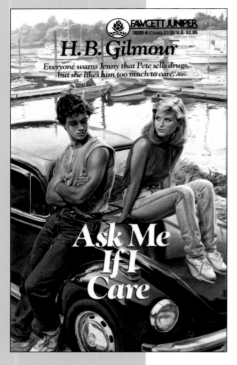

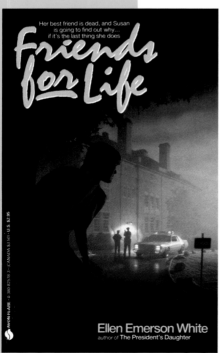

a stone-cold-sober protagonist who is forced to journey to the seedy, drug-ridden underbelly of someplace or another to find a loved one; in Susan Dodson's 1982 book *Have You Seen This Girl?*, 16-year-old Tom runs away to New York City in search of his girlfriend who had become an addict, and in Ellen Emerson White's 1983 novel *Friends for Life*, high-schooler Susan attempts to solve the mystery of her best friend Colleen's suspicious fatal LSD overdose by going undercover with the school drug crowd and eventually discovering that the school preppies are PCP-smoking murderers (what else is new, right?).

But antidrug novels came back in a big way in the late '90s—perhaps in response to a surge in heroin use after the drug became cheaper, purer, more readily available, and even more fashionable (see: the heroin chic trend and its emaciated models). The critical and commercial success of British author Melvin Burgess's *Smack*, a love story first published in 1996 about two teen runaways who become addicted to heroin and get in trouble with the law, might also have kickstarted the wave of latter-day antidrug books. These included Cynthia D. Grant's *The White Horse* and Linda Glovach's *Beauty Queen*, both anti-heroin novels published in 1998. Glovach has long been rumored to have played a role in writing *Go Ask Alice*, which might explain why *Beauty*

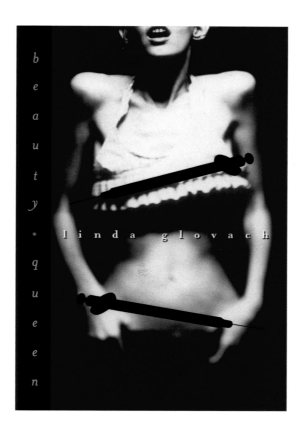

beauty * queen

linda glovach

Artsy, photographic, and pretty much as graphic as you can get on a YA cover—yes, those are syringes—the cover of *Beauty Queen* makes it clear that, despite its innocuous title, this is a book about drugs.

Queen is almost exactly the same book. Though *Beauty Queen*'s Sam comes from rougher circumstances than the middle-class protagonist of *Alice*—she has an alcoholic mom, a creepy stepdad, and a depressing job at a strip club—this diary-style book follows a similar trajectory. Sam accepts an offer of heroin from one of her strip club coworkers, is instantly addicted, and is soon dead. And though *Beauty Queen* doesn't claim to be a real diary, Glovach writes on the book's back cover that "writing the book, I saw my old dope dealer and bought $1,500 worth of pure heroin—Brown Gold—and started shooting up 10 times a day to get the feel of the book…but I'm off it for good." Helluva way to just say no—and also a pretty grabby marketing blurb.

The Murder of Kaitlyn Arquette

One of the most celebrated authors of teen thrillers, Lois Duncan wrote from the '50s through the '90s, putting out YA classics like *I Know What You Did Last Summer* and *Stranger with My Face* (see page 217). But, as her official website notes, "the most difficult book Lois Duncan ever had to write was non-fiction."

That book was 1992's *Who Killed My Daughter?*, which focused on the unsolved 1989 murder of Duncan's 18-year-old daughter, Kaitlyn Arquette. Law enforcement in Albuquerque, New Mexico, where the family resided, pronounced it an awful accident: Kaitlyn, in the wrong place at the wrong time, was killed in a drive-by shooting while driving her car downtown. But Duncan came to believe otherwise.

Feeling ignored by local police, Duncan began working with several psychics, one of whom concluded that Kaitlyn's boyfriend, who was later found to be involved in a complex insurance fraud enterprise, knew what really happened. Duncan also came to believe that her book *Don't Look Behind You*, which was unpublished at the time of Kaitlyn's death, foreshadowed the murder; the main character was modeled on Kaitlyn, one real-life suspect shared a name with the book's villain, and a sketch drawn by one of the psychics she consulted looked like the depiction of the villain on the book's UK cover illustration.

Despite its extremely grim subject matter (and unfortunate moments of racism, particularly in regards to Kaitlyn's boyfriend, who was a Vietnamese refugee), *Who Killed My Daughter?* was named a Best Book of the Year by *School Library Journal* and a Best Book for Young Adults by the American Library Association. In a review written at the time of publication, *Publishers Weekly* noted that "readers critical of either Duncan's contacts with paranormals or her talking to God and to her dead daughter may be put off by the book, but many will be sympathetic to this mother's plight."

After Kaitlyn's death Duncan turned away from the genre that made her famous, publishing only one more YA book, *Gallows Hill*, in 1997, which she struggled to complete. "I went weak after Kait's murder," Lois told Tim Stelloh of *BuzzFeed* in 2014. "How could I even think about creating a novel with a young woman in a life-threatening situation?" But she kept writing books, including *One to the Wolves: On the Trail of a Killer*, the 2013 sequel to

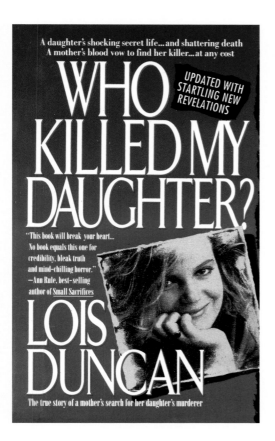

A daughter's shocking secret life...and shattering death
A mother's blood vow to find her killer...at any cost

WHO KILLED MY DAUGHTER?

UPDATED WITH STARTLING NEW REVELATIONS

"This book will break your heart... No book equals this one for credibility, bleak truth and mind-chilling horror."
—Ann Rule, best-selling author of Small Sacrifices

LOIS DUNCAN

The true story of a mother's search for her daughter's murderer

Though Lois Duncan wrote novels almost exclusively for a teenage audience, the cover of her nonfiction title is styled in keeping with most first-person, true crime books for adults— certainly to differentiate this book from the rest of her list, and possibly to attract a new, grown-up readership who hadn't heard of her fiction.

Who Killed My Daughter?. In it she documents her life in the two decades following the publication of first book, when she worked with private eyes and appeared on TV in hopes of drawing attention to Kaitlyn's case. She also maintained a now-defunct website called Real Crimes, which was dedicated to the stories of unsolved murders like Kaitlyn's.

The Albuquerque police eventually charged two men with Kaitlyn's death, claiming that they had planned the murder to look like a random drive-by shooting, but the charges were dismissed. When Duncan died in 2016, Kaitlyn's murder was still an open investigation—one that Duncan had never abandoned. As she told Susan Schindehette of *People* magazine in 1997, "In dreams, Kaitlyn tells me, 'Don't give up, mother.' It's not a matter of revenge. It's a matter of Kait being worth the truth."

A Very Special ~~Episode~~ Paperback

In the '80s, a number of teen suicide "clusters," the most infamous of which unfolded in Bergenfield, New Jersey, in 1987, made Americans sit up and pay attention to their children's mental health. Not all the attention was helpful; a 1987 *New York Times* article on teen suicide blames divorce and "the playthings of the 1980's: personal computers, VCR's and stereos." But even though some were misguided, adults were more interested in the inner torments their kids experienced than ever before.

At the same time, vicious crimes committed by teens, like the 1984 drug-and-Satanism-fueled murder committed by New Jersey teen Ricky Kasso or Anthony Jacques Broussard's 1981 murder of his high school classmate Marcy Conrad, whose dead body he then showed off to friends, convinced many adults that they didn't understand teens and their motivations as well as they thought they did.

So it makes sense that a subset of '80s and '90s problem novels feature teens engaging in all manner of violent acts—suicide, assault, murder. In addition to graphic, ripped-from-the-headlines content, these stories are also marked by their lack of tidy resolutions. Ultimately, the young characters did unthinkably violent things not because their families had fractured or society had not lived up to its promises but . . . well, just because they did. According to Deborah Stevenson, director of the Center for Children's Books at the University of Illinois at Urbana-Champaign, one of the differences between '70s YA and '80s YA is what constitutes an ending: many '70s problem novels were wrapped up with a clear conclusion, or what Stevenson describes as the "'and Jennifer finally told a teacher. Whew! The end.' conclusion." In the novels of the '80s, endings got a lot more equivocal.

That's certainly the case in some of the era's more highbrow novels about troubled teens, like Richard Peck's 1985 teen suicide drama *Remembering the Good Times* and Robert Cormier's *We All Fall Down* from 1991, which details a gang's violent, nihilistic attack on a family home and, eventually, the family's youngest daughter. But the move away from easy answers was just as common in less prestigious novels; in this era, there was often little difference between the "issues" novels that got a librarian seal of approval and those that didn't. Especially when it came to violence, most authors seemed bent on discussing distressing events in as sensitive a fashion as possible.

Books that focused on teens who turned their violence outward offered similarly open endings. In Susan Beth Pfeffer's 1980 novel *About David*, Lynn is understandably shocked and confused when she learns that her oldest friend, David, has killed not only himself

but also his aggressive, bullying parents. She hopes that reading David's journals will bring her peace, and though they offer some insight into David's state of mind, they don't help her understand why he did what he did. Lynn's life only begins to return to normal once she realizes that the truth of why David killed his family is beyond her and that the only choice she can make is to keep living.

Not all books avoided explaining the horrors that tenth graders are capable of. Steven Kroll's 1986 novel *Breaking Camp* tried hard to provide answers, which might be why the book ultimately comes up short. Ted goes to an all-boys horseback-riding camp, to enjoy such innocent, all-American pastimes as hard work, the pursuit of excellence, and horses. But he soon finds that the camp is also full of wealthy lunatic bullies who are psyched about hazing other campers. Not innocent, all-American hazing, like forcing someone to drink

With its leaping flames and dead-simple tagline, *Breaking Camp*'s drama is literally out in the open.

milk till they spew, mind you; I'm talking about stealing the hazing victims' clothes, locking them in a fort filled with manure, making them bite on wooden bits, and poking them with cattle prods. (Yes, I'm serious.) The adults at the camp, of course, turn a blind eye.

Breaking Camp is not quite Robert Cormier's *The Chocolate War*, that high-water mark in examining pointless teen male-on-teen male violence. It's never clear exactly what status quo the camp bullies are trying to protect, and the book's attempt to explain how things got so out of hand falls flat: "I guess when you can do anything you want and a certain kind of attitude supports you, there's always the temptation to go one step further." That might be a decent explanation of, say, the Trump administration, but it hardly explains how a bunch of average-seeming boys became mini Marquis de Sades. *Breaking Camp*'s most lasting value might be in showing why trying to tidily explain the cruelty of which teens are capable is a fool's errand.

Issues novels had better luck trying to make sense of "new" problems, like eating disorders. In 1978, when therapist Steven Levenkron's novel about a young ballet dancer with anorexia, *The Best Little Girl in the World*, became a hit, many Americans learned about—or put a name to—the disease for the first time. In 1983, the anorexia-related death of musician Karen Carpenter made eating disorders a national concern, which helped expand the eating disorder novel into a veritable YA subgenre. Books like Levenkron's 1986 sequel *Kessa*, Rebecca Josephs's 1980 novel *Early Disorder*, and Anne Snyder's 1980 book *Goodbye, Paper Doll*, followed a certain structure: a beautiful white teen girl struggles with an eating disorder and becomes dangerously underweight. Then, something pushes her onto the road to recovery. In *Early*, it's the death of the protagonist's friend from anorexia complications; in *Kessa*, the heroine, who successfully completed treatment for her eating disorder in *Best Little Girl*, works through a relapse with the help of a therapist.

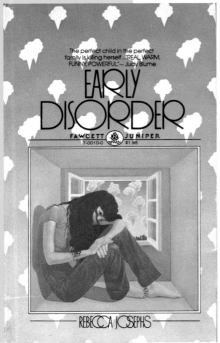

The vast majority of the era's eating disorder novels suffers from similar issues. Not only did these stories often oversimplify the nature of eating disorders, but they featured exclusively only white female protagonists, thus furthering the pernicious myth that these deadly conditions affect only white women and girls. Virginia Hamilton's *Cousins* (page 111) is one rare exception: one of the protagonists, Patty Ann, is an African American teen who is battling bulimia and who is not defined solely by her disease.

But not all authors became more sensitive in handling taboo topics. Look no further than Beatrice Sparks, a youth counselor who shot to fame as the "editor" (read: ghostwriter) of *Go Ask Alice* and who never met a cultural calamity she couldn't cash in on. In 1971, it was drugs and *Alice*; in 1978, it was the teen Satanic panic and *Jay's Journal*, which, like *Alice*, tells the story of a teen's descent into darkness through diary form. With *Jay's Journal*, however, Sparks ran into trouble. The novel is based on the real diaries of a depressed teen who committed suicide;

With its type-laden cover, *Kessa* doesn't hold back on drama—the shout-outs to the media tie-ins and the all-bold, all-red ANOREXIA NERVOSA create a distinctly tabloidy feel. *Early Disorder*, on the other hand, takes a more serious approach with a Magritte-meets-Peter Max cloud pattern and a quote from Judy Blume.

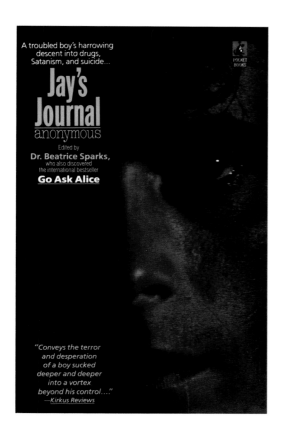

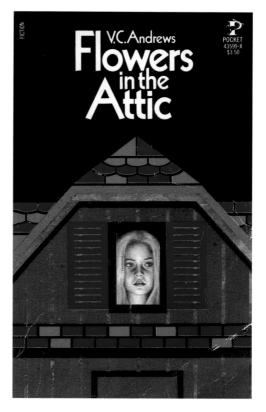

his mother, who shared them with Sparks, hoped to inspire another cautionary tale. Instead, Sparks wrote a book in which "anti-war hippie" morphed into a blood-drinking, kitten-killing, violent-orgy-having Satanist who allows himself to be possessed by a demonic spirit called Raul. Sparks continued to pump out sensationalistic books through the '90s (see page 199), but although she hopped from parental worry to parental worry, she never absorbed that genuine empathy for teens was the new major trend.

Besides the obviously taboo subject material, part of the "forbidden book" allure of *Flowers in the Attic* was that it was originally published for adults, not teens. *Jay's Journal*, on the other hand, had the kind of dire messaging that might also draw in the occasional overprotective parent reader.

Luckily, more sensitivity was typically present in the era's wave of books about sexual assault. Not all of them, of course—V. C. Andrews's *Flowers in the Attic* famously broached the taboo subject of incest in 1979, but its approach was more Gothic than realistic (not to mention queasily voyeuristic rather than frank about the consequences of such abuse). But when stories about the violent assaults of older teens—usually committed by acquaintances or strangers—entered the YA mainstream in the mid to late '70s, they were usually handled thoughtfully, as in books like Richard Peck's *Are You Alone in the House?* (see page 178), Sandra Scoppettone's *Happy Endings Are All Alike* (see page 31), and Gloria D. Miklowitz's *Did You Hear What Happened to Andrea?* from 1979. And in the '80s and '90s, that sensitivity was turned onto the sexual abuse of younger children as well.

Laura Nathanson's 1986 book *The Trouble with Wednesdays* tells the story of Becky, a 12-year-old who descends into depression, shame, and rage after her orthodontist begins molesting her. The adults around her eventually discover the abuse—but not before she's suffered a great deal. A few years later, in 1993, Cynthia D. Grant's *Uncle Vampire* ushered in a trend of similarly themed novels focused on the tale of a teenager who is sexually assaulted by a male relative. In Grant's story, Carolyn has been abused by her uncle almost her entire life and retreats into a world of fantasy (in which he is a "vampire" who visits her and her twin at night) to try to cope. In 1994, the Violence Against Women Act was finally passed and the Rape, Abuse, & Incest National Network (RAINN) was founded, but these books were just ahead of the curve; these titles made it possible for abuse survivors to pop into the teen section of their local library and, in those pre-internet years, finally learn that they were not alone.

The Trouble with Wednesdays

Laura Nathanson

CYNTHIA D. GRANT

UNCLE VAMPIRE

There's no easy way to illustrate a cover about sexual abuse—too scary, and no kid will pick it up; too lurid, and no adult will put it in a school library—and hedging your bets with something neutral can lead to a nasty bait-and-switch for the reader. *Uncle Vampire* uses the menacing background to indicate that this isn't fun (and isn't about vampires), while *The Trouble with Wednesdays* contrasts the goofy and innocent Tommy the Tooth poster with a visibly distressed protagonist.

Sick Lit Criticism

Lurlene McDaniel may be the queen of the subgenre, but books about teens and tweens with serious illness and/or disability are still YA mainstays, from *Wonder* to *The Fault in Our Stars* to *Everything, Everything*. Although long marketed as books about tweens who learn about illness and develop empathy, such stories often promote harmful ideas about illness and disability. As Jessie Male, a writer and disability studies scholar, told me, "Books by authors like Lurlene McDaniel lack what my writing mentor calls 'the piss and the shit' of the story."

In stories like these, Male explained, illness is cleaned up and made pretty: "the aftermath of a procedure might be described, like the placement of a wig, but there wasn't description of chemotherapy, and the pain that happens throughout the body during these treatments." There is also a tendency, she noted, to "treat illness as metaphor for strength," despite the fact that in real life, "suffering, perhaps, doesn't build character. Sometimes suffering is just that—pain; distress."

Male knows what she's talking about from more than just a scholarly perspective; she read McDaniel's books as a tween. "There is a romanticism attached to illness in McDaniel's stories, and as a young teenager . . . this was the major appeal," said Male. "It was a time in my life where I was discovering my sexuality, and this was a very safe way to explore this, because—at least in the texts from the 1990s—there wasn't any sex."

Teen illness books have changed. As Male noted, "I think they've certainly become less chaste! And the YA genre has become more diverse in relation to race, sexuality, and ability." But they haven't all confronted the problems the genre had in the '80s and '90s. "I'd argue that the most popular stories—and these are also those often picked up for cinematic adaptation—are those that perpetuate dangerous and inaccurate representations of illness and disability," said Male. "*The Fault in Our Stars* is the perfect example of this. Here, one disabled character, who dies, becomes the source of another's growth.

"And although YA texts in general are more diverse, the main characters in illness narratives are often white, middle and upper class, and straight. . . . What does this say about who is being recognized? This is a reflection on the American health care system in general, where the stories of women of color are not often recognized, or even believed."

In Sickness and In Sickness

Children dealing with illness have always had a home in kid lit; as early as 1872, books like *What Katy Did*, which followed the titular 12-year-old she recovered from a spinal injury, dealt with grave matters of sickness and health, with varying degrees of sensitivity. (In *Katy*, the heroine's injury is basically blamed on her having a bad attitude; this definitely falls on the bottom of that sensitivity scale.) But the popular culture of the '70s saw a surge in stories about illness, largely ushered in by Erich Segal's 1970 novel *Love Story*. The source of every vapid popular girl's yearbook quote "Love means never having to say you're sorry," *Love Story* portrays the romance between young couple Oliver and Jenny, which ends when Jenny suddenly dies from leukemia. The megahit book became a wildly popular film the same year and spawned other media about illness, including the 1976 made-for-TV movie *The Boy in the Plastic Bubble*, which featured a young John Travolta as a teenager with a severely impaired immune system.

Nevertheless, it was in the '80s that this subgenre of YA truly caught fire. Children's book publisher Willowisp even had an imprint called Lifelines that, according to a publisher description, put out novels that "depict characters dealing with life-threatening situations are very popular with the middle- and high-school reader." Lifelines' titles more than lived up to that description; among them were *Is My Sister Dying?* (1991) and *Is Chelsea Going Blind?* (1986) by Alida E. Young, *When Mirrors Lie* by Isaacsen-Bright (1984), and *Now That Andi's Gone* by Karle Dickerson (1994).

Though illness stories were myriad, one writer's name has become synonymous with books about sick teens. Lurlene McDaniel jokingly told *Publishers Weekly*'s Kate Pavao that in the '90s librarians referred to her as "the crying-and-dying lady," but in fact it's not much of a joke. McDaniel tried out more conventional YA fare early on in her career (like her 1982 book *Miss Teen: I'm a Cover Girl*

Lifelines

Now That Andi's Gone

KARLE DICKERSON

ONE LAST WISH

Lurlene McDaniel

A Season for Goodbye

Now!), but found success with stories about illness and death, like *Six Months to Live* in 1985, *I Want to Live* in 1987, *Goodbye Doesn't Mean Forever* and *Too Young to Die* in 1989, and her One Last Wish series, which debuted in 1995. In the McDaniel formula, a sweet, virginal, and (usually) white female protagonist is under the care of a godlike doctor who makes all the decisions about treatment. She has a "healthy" best friend and may become romantically involved with a boy who is also battling illness (but she is totally, utterly not interested in sex). While McDaniel's books take place in contemporary times, they bear strong overtones to Victorian literature about angelic young women who fall ill and suffer heroically and then inspire the people around them to better themselves (think Beth in *Little Women*), a theme that's arguably part and parcel of the everything-old-is-new-again family-values culture of the '80s.

Lurlene McDaniel

I Want to Live

A companion to
Six Months to Live

Despite their anodyne-bordering-on-treacly tone, McDaniel's novels still provoke heated debates to this day. McDaniel boosters argue that her books educate readers about modern medicine (she works with medical professionals and hospice organizations to make sure that her books are medically accurate), and occasionally spur fans towards lives of altruism; according to a 2013 profile of McDaniel, *Six Months to Live* inspired at least one fan to go to medical school. Critics say she perpetuates harmful ideas about illness and disability.

Of course, McDaniel wasn't the only YA author to write about teens with illnesses. Jennifer Baker's 1994 series Last Summer, First Love documented a young girl navigating her first serious relationship while dealing with lupus, and Cherie Bennett's Surviving

SHE THOUGHT SHE'D FOUND LOVE...
BUT INSTEAD LOST HER LIFE TO AIDS
It happened to Nancy
by an
ANONYMOUS TEENAGER
A TRUE STORY
FROM HER DIARY

16 series, which ran briefly from 1993 to 1994, told stories of hot popular girls dealing with sudden illnesses, to name just a few. Deeply flawed as they may be, McDaniel's work and similar illness melodramas have more to offer besides a solid weep and some very problematic ideas. Yes, they are far from perfect, and often exploitative and disempowering to those with illness. But their popularity pointed to a burning desire among young women to grapple with big questions of life and death, illness and health—a desire that modern YA tries to address more thoughtfully and with greater nuance.

As anyone who lived through the era can tell you, these two decades were marked by a culture-wide obsession with two illnesses in particular: HIV and AIDS. Unfortunately, this meant that the field of teen HIV literature was wide open for over-the-top sensationalists like Beatrice Sparks, who pivoted to innocent teen victims in her next "anonymous" "diary," *It Happened to Nancy,* in 1994. Fourteen-year-old Nancy, like all Sparks protagonists, is both naive and incredibly unlucky, and after she meets her first love at a Garth Brooks concert, he quickly drugs and sexually assaults her (which Nancy describes as "committing fornication on my mother's own bed"). Soon after, she learns that she has contracted HIV. Nancy keeps a stiff upper lip while suffering through gruesome complications, and like McDaniel's heroines, she focuses on staying positive and finding love with a popular boy who promises they'll save sex until they're married. *Nancy*'s warning reaches much further than *Go Ask Alice* or *Jay's Journal*; instead of caution-ing teens about drugs or Satanism, Sparks seems to be implying that even innocent open-mouthed kissing can end in ruin.

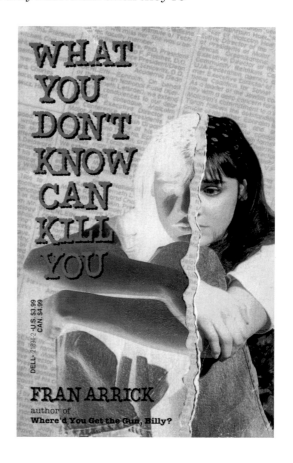

Luckily, Sparks wasn't the only YA author to address HIV during the '90s. Fran Arrick, a pseudonym of YA author Judie Angell, tackled many big problems throughout her career,

The cover of *What You Don't Know Can Kill You* takes a very literal approach to "ripped from the headlines" by, well, ripping up some headlines. But rather than make the plot feel tabloidesque, the newspaper elements evoke the external, media-driven perception of AIDS—and how it surrounds, and weighs on, protagonist Ellen.

like antisemitism (1982's *Chernowitz*), the sexual exploitation of minors (1978's *Steffie Can't Come Out to Play*; see page 174) and gun violence (1991's *Where'd You Get the Gun, Billy?*). Her 1992 HIV drama *What You Don't Know Can Kill You* is one of the small handful of '90s YA novels that examines heterosexual, middle-class women and HIV transmission—and unlike *It Happened to Nancy*, it doesn't imply that HIV is the natural consequence of refusing to sign a purity pledge. Like most YA heroines, high school senior Ellen is pretty, popular, and in love with her hunky boyfriend, a college freshman. Unlike most YA heroines, she's crazy-psyched about running the school blood drive! But when the blood Ellen donates tests positive for HIV, she learns that her boyfriend had contracted HIV and passed it on to her during one of their few sexual encounters.

What You Don't Know Can Kill You certainly isn't perfect, and it has its shame-y and overblown moments ("You were away from home for the first time, some guys handed you a bottle and some laughs, and what did you get? Some death!" Ellen's boyfriend muses dramatically at one point). But compared to the pearl-clutching "What had she done to deserve such a terrible sentence as AIDS?" in *Sixteen and Dying* or *Nancy*'s hand-wringing about "committing fornication," Ellen's story, while melodramatic, is told with more sensitivity than its contemporaries. Perhaps most important, Ellen is no victim, like Nancy or countless other similar characters; instead, she's determined to be independent and fully embrace the life she has left.

More manageable chronic illnesses turned up in a few titles, too, most famously in *Baby-Sitters Club #3: The Truth about Stacey* (see page 145) but also in lesser known books like Patricia Hermes's *What If They Knew?* from 1980. Ten-year-old heroine Jeremy fears that if her classmates found out about her epilepsy, they'd ostracize her. So she keeps her disorder a secret, until she is blackmailed by a cruel and ableist school bully, who steals her medication (!). Jeremy

<blockquote>
79515 • U.S. $2.25
CAN. $2.95

A DELL YEARLING BOOK

Does Jeremy really have something to hide?

WHAT IF THEY KNEW?

Patricia Hermes
</blockquote>

The cover of *What If They Knew?* doesn't hint at darkness or cruelty. In fact, the illustration makes it seem more like a friendship book about gossipy pals. The tagline mentions the "secret" but doesn't quite reveal the bullying that the novel contains.

then has a seizure at school and finds that her friends still like her, and despite her bully's best efforts, Jeremy ends up just fine, happy and secure in her friendships. Like Stacey, she's almost the anti-McDaniel heroine: a girl with an illness who has no interest in being a perfect angel and just wants to be herself.

First Comes Love, Then Comes . . . Some Other Stuff

Even with contemporary social issues constantly entering the YA mainstream throughout the '80s and '90s, the genre still had room for the classics, such as teen pregnancy novels. In fact, YA and cultural concerns about teen pregnancy have always been intertwined, because they were born (sorry!) at the same time.

American teenagers were giving birth at unprecedented rates in the '50s and '60s, and teen pregnancy was declared a social menace. So of course, pregnancy quickly found its way into books written for young people. Early books about teen pregnancy generally explored the three options available at the time: marrying the boy who knocked you up (as seen in 1967's *Mr. and Mrs. Bo Jo Jones*), staying at a group home for pregnant teens until you give birth and your child is adopted by people who are better than you, you dirty, sinful girl (as seen in 1971's *Girls of Huntington House*), or not marrying the boy who knocked you up and becoming the dread *Unwed Mother* (1974), a term that shot to popularity in the 1960s, as did those groovy bellbottoms that protagonist Kathy wears on the book's cover. It was a depressing set of choices, which reflected the depressing reality that most pregnant girls were living with at the time (although, again, these books almost exclusively featured white heroines).

Then circumstances changed for American women—in 1972, Title IX ensured that pregnant teens had the right to attend school, and the Supreme Court's ruling on 1973's *Roe v. Wade* **case** guaranteed that women in the U.S. had the legal right to terminate pregnancies if they chose—and YA novels changed with them. Abortion became a more common topic, and books began to acknowledge that teen parents could have lives outside changing diapers and repenting for their lusty ways.

Though she's not as well known today, Norma Klein was sort

TEMPO BOOKS $1.50 12951

Kathy was only fifteen
but she knew what she wanted—
to keep her baby!

Unwed Mother

—a novel by
Gloria D. Miklowitz

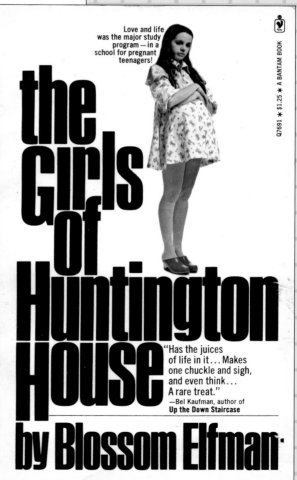

Love and life
was the major study
program—in a
school for pregnant
teenagers!

Q7691 ★ $1.25 ★ A BANTAM BOOK

the Girls of Huntington House

"Has the juices
of life in it... Makes
one chuckle and sigh,
and even think...
A rare treat."
—Bel Kaufman, author of
Up the Down Staircase

by Blossom Elfman

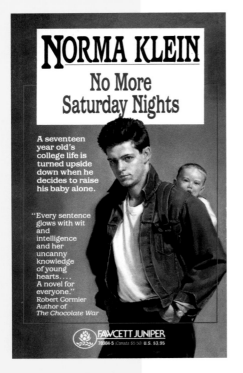

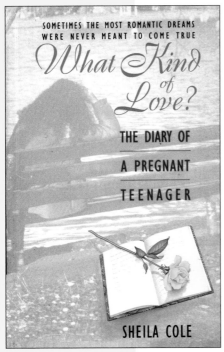

of the Xtina to Judy Blume's Britney; they rose to the top of YA simultaneously in the '70s and '80s, offering variations on the theme of teen girls exploring their sexuality. Klein specialized in sexually knowing, urban teen sophisticates who were far more likely to complain to their mothers about their European lover's unusually dense foreskin than to name a penis "Ralph." But Klein (whose books were banned as often as Blume's in the '70s and '80s) didn't get racy for raciness's sake. She dealt with the tough emotional issues around sexuality, too, such as teen parenthood, as in her 1988 book *No More Saturday Nights*. Protagonist Tim has scored a real hat trick of YA misery: his mother is dead, he and his father can barely communicate, and a tryst with classmate Cheryl has made him a father himself at 18 years old. Cheryl wants to sell their baby to a childless couple, prompting a judge to award custody to Tim, who, though jobless and about to leave town to attend Columbia University, isn't trying to turn a quick buck with his progeny.

Baby in tow, Tim shows up at Columbia, where he learns that, yes, being a teen dad who is also attending one of the most prestigious universities in the world is tough. He juggles baby, classes, sitters, and his cadre of female roommates (one of whom he hooks up with). But he also repairs his relationship with his father and decides

that being a full-time student/dad is kind of his thing. *Saturday Nights* is unusual in its focus on a single dad, rather than the teen mothers of earlier books, and it is also indicative of a new trend in teen parent novels: though we never learn exactly what made Tim interested in being a single teen dad in the first place, we see that his pursuit of his hopes and his plans for the future hasn't come to an abrupt stop just because he has a kid.

This is not to say that the '90s wanted for teen mother stories. *What Kind of Love?: The Diary of a Pregnant Teenager*, a 1995 book by Sheila Cole, brings us Valerie, a popular 15-year-old who is in love with her boyfriend, Peter. In the grand tradition of the sensationalist teen pregnancy novel, she gets her positive pregnancy test, immediately finds out that she and Peter aren't actually in love, and then realizes that her popularity was contingent on not being visibly pregnant, all in short order. The rawness of Valerie's emotions—she's not just sad about her situation, she's pissed and lost—represent a break with the genre's tradition, but her options, either to run off with Peter or give her baby up for adoption, nonetheless feel retro.

Even before the *Roe v. Wade* decision, there was, of course, a fourth option. Paul Zindel's 1969 book *My Darling, My Hamburger*, widely thought to be the first YA novel to deal with abortion, delivers a template for the "abortion as punishment" story: the protagonist gets pregnant, is dumped by her jerk boyfriend, spends prom night getting an abortion, doesn't attend graduation, and by the end of the novel refuses to speak to her best friend. Judy Blume has famously said that she wrote *Forever*... after her daughter asked for "a story about two nice kids who have sex without either of them having to die," because, at the time, the heroines who tried to get abortions in '60s and '70s YA novels regularly met dire fates. These punishments rolled on through the early years of the problem novel, such as in Jeanette Eyerly's 1972 *Bonnie Jo, Go Home*, in which the titular character loses her virginity to a random jerk, becomes

Sean and Liz and Dennis and Maggie! Senior year isn't the end of high school— it's the beginning of Life!

My Darling, My Hamburger

A novel by

Paul Zindel

Author of *Pardon Me, You're Stepping On My Eyeball!*

11605-3 ★ $1.75 ★ A BANTAM BOOK

pregnant, then travels to New York for a traumatic abortion. To be fair, many pre-Roe abortions *were* horribly traumatic, but in these books, they became the entire story, eclipsing anything else about the heroine or the life she might lead afterward.

In 1973, the year Roe was decided, *Growing Up in a Hurry* by Winifred Madison was published, in which the heroine actually grows closer to her emotionally distant mother after she asks for her help getting a safe abortion. Yet change, in plotlines and in cultural attitudes, was slow; Gallup polls show that support for abortion rights remained fairly consistent between 1975 and 1990, with numbers dropping just a little in the early '80s. Abortion problem novels remained stuck in one of two main categories: positively pro-choice, or old-school abortion-as-punishment gorefest.

Ann Rinaldi's 1982 book *Promises Are for Keeping* is one of the latter. The main narrative focuses on Nicki, a strong-willed orphan being raised by her two older brothers, and the abortion comes into play after her best friend, Meredith, has sex in order to please her boyfriend. Nikki has been stealing birth control pills from her doctor brother to give to Meredith, but fears that if her brother thought the pills were for her, he would "force her to resign as class yearbook photographer and miss the Saturday football games." That makes perfect sense—who among us *hasn't* gotten pregnant at a Saturday football game? Of course, Meredith becomes pregnant anyway, and despite living in a post-Roe world, her

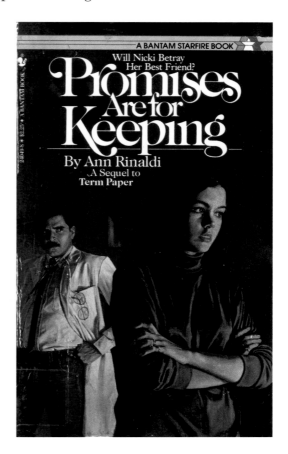

abortion goes wrong. Nicki's doctor brother swoops in and save Meredith's life, but he can't save her uterus. Meredith's moment of feeling even the slightest sense of agency about her body is punished with a hysterectomy. No editorializing—she actually calls the surgery her "punishment."

Luckily, not every YA book about abortion from that time reads like an entry in Mike Pence's dream journal. A. M. Stephensen's 1982 novel *Unbirthday* has an admittedly uncomfortable title for a book about abortion. It's also short on plot: Louisa accidentally becomes pregnant while having sex with her extremely supportive boyfriend, weighs her options, and decides to get an abortion. But it makes up for it in clarity, walking readers through not only every step of the abortion procedure, but also how to find an abortion

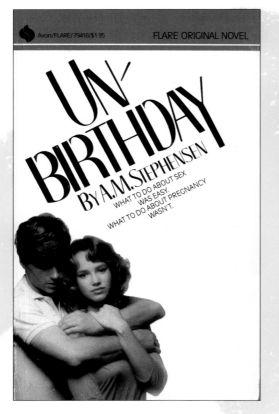

provider, how to prepare for a pelvic exam, and where to get sympathetic support (Louisa finds a feminist shoulder to cry on at the local college women's center). It's not just a story to reveal the logistics of abortion to girls who can't find *Our Bodies, Ourselves* at Waldenbooks, though. Louisa feels no guilt about her choice and also specifically calls out the melodrama of abortion novels: "There was only one book I could remember where a girl got an abortion. It was so badly botched that she ended up puking blood all over the upholstery of her boyfriend's car on the way home." Lacking role models, as many girls at the time did, Louisa decides to become one herself, and in doing so, becomes one for her readers.

Norma Klein also fought antiabortion stigma with 1983's *Beginner's Love*, though with a bit more style than *Unbirthday*. Leda and Joel are, like all Klein characters, way hipper as high schoolers than we'll ever be (for example: when they meet, Leda is wearing a button that says "Castrate Rapists"). They embark on their first serious relationship, lose their virginity together, and eventually deal with an accidental pregnancy. Joel and Leda calmly discuss their options, both knowing that having a kid is not in the cards right now. Leda gets an abortion and that's the end of it—no complications, hysterectomies, or over-the-top grief. When they drift apart afterward, there's neither finger-pointing nor the implication that Leda is broken. Rather, the abortion seems to have simply exposed a hole in their high school relationship, and they both go on to happy, normal lives in college.

Blume gets the glory, but Klein, who passed away in 1989, did as much to push YA to its limits, and it's perhaps the more complicated messages of her work that make her less widely hailed. Judy's girls found pleasure in their bodies; Norma's girls learned that bodies were sites of both pleasure and pain, but also that they were absolutely their own.

CHAPTER 7

Terror

STALKERS,

SLASHERS,

and

FREAKY

CHILD GHOSTS

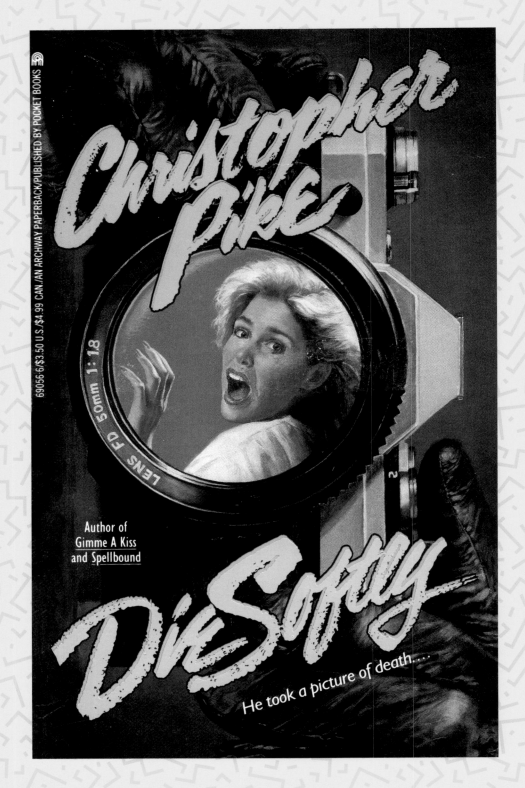

Christopher Pike

69056-6/$3.50 U.S./$4.99 CAN./AN ARCHWAY PAPERBACK/PUBLISHED BY POCKET BOOKS

LENS FD 50mm 1:1.8

Author of
Gimme A Kiss
and Spellbound

Die Softly

He took a picture of death....

Teens and monsters go together like immortal bloodsuckers and virginal heroines. By the 1950s, when teen culture was in full swing, horror stories were everywhere in America: the decade saw the tail end of the Universal monster movie craze that brought us *Frankenstein, The Wolf Man,* and, less memorably, *The Leech Woman,* as well as the brief reign of EC Comics, the pulp comic book publisher of *Tales from the Crypt.* These horror concepts were almost immediately injected into the emerging teen media landscape, with 1957's *I Was a Teenage Werewolf* leading a pack of teen monster movies that included *I Was a Teenage Frankenstein, Teenage Zombies, Teenagers from Outer Space, Teenage Monster,* and more.

But these films weren't just about Dracula going to gym class. They also illuminated how vulnerable to harm teens were. In these movies, adults tend not only to ignore the problems of adolescence but to exacerbate them. As media scholar Cyndy Hendershot wrote in her 2001 *Images Journal* article "Monster at the Soda Shop: Teenagers and Fifties Horror Films": "authority frequently does not so much fail, but willfully creates monsters."

But while horror was almost instantly part of teen cinema, teen literature took another few decades to pick up the baton. In mid-century malt shop novels, the closest thing to horror was someone wearing white after Labor Day. Mystery series like Nancy Drew occasionally got spooky, and writers like Lois Duncan and Willo

Davis Roberts had been writing supernatural suspense novels for younger audiences since before the dawn of disco, but YA horror truly peaked in the '80s. By that point, YA had been cooking for a few years, horror had become a bona fide phenomenon in adult publishing, with *The Exorcist* (1971), *The Shining* (1977), and their imitators burning up best-seller lists, and teen horror movies had come back in vogue beginning with 1978's *Halloween*.

Dell launched the teen supernatural horror line Twilight: Where Darkness Begins in 1982, which was followed by Bantam's extremely similar Dark Forces line in 1983. Both series featured teen heroes battling stuff like evil ghost twins and demonic dollhouses. But in 1985 Christopher Pike's *Slumber Party* was published, kicking off the mania for slasher-style teen horror thrillers.

What followed was an avalanche of books whose cover illustrations (and plots) mimicked *Halloween* and *Nightmare on Elm Street* and *Friday the 13th*. After he published several successful stand-alone horror novels in this vein, R. L. Stine jump-scared his Fear Street series in 1989, creating the era's first blockbuster horror series; fellow Stine horror behemoth Goosebumps followed in 1992. In 1991, the era's other famous horror line, Scholastic's Point Horror, was founded, and the trend was on fire. As Michael Cart, former president of the Young Adult Library Services Association, wrote in *From Romance to Realism: 50 Years of Growth and Change in Young Adult Literature*, "the paperback horror novel became to publishing in the nineties what romance paperbacks had been to the eighties."

Though the decade's most high-profile YA horror drew from ultra-violent films, other books skewed softer, showing supernatural creatures not only as unthreatening, but as beings who could improve humans' lives. This empathy (and, okay, horniness) for monsters laid the groundwork for Twilight, *Buffy the Vampire Slayer*, and an entire generation predisposed to understand (and, okay, be horny for) misunderstood creatures of the night.

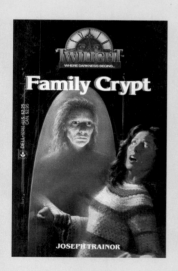

A Ghost Ate My Homework

In our culture, we tend to assume that young people can deal with the uglier side of life only if there's an unreal, mystical gloss on the whole thing. This is why our parents let us watch the David Bowie–rific fantasy kidnapping classic *Labyrinth* in elementary school, but not documentaries about the Lindbergh baby. And, like Virgil to a child's Dante, ghost characters can provide a comforting presence in the face of frightening concepts like death, betrayal, the multiple secret passageways in your new house, and so on. From the 1939 storybook that gave the world Casper the Friendly Ghost (and his various competitors, such as the extremely-not-copyright-violating 1962 picture book *Gus Was a Friendly Ghost*) onward, ghost-child pairings have been popular throughout the past century-plus of English literature.

Yet ghosts—even affable ones!—were not initially an important part of teen novels. Although the supernatural played well with younger kids, it didn't click with early YA's emphasis on realism. Even adventure and mystery books for adolescent readers that existed before YA qua YA generally incorporated the supernatural into plots only to prove that the supernatural did not actually exist. For example, in Nancy Drew's 1948 adventure *The Ghost of Blackwood Hall*, the ghosts are so fake that the idiots who believe they are real are preyed upon by heartless criminals.

A sea change came in the '80s, when realistic middle grade and YA fiction ran head-on into an overarching trend of spooky entertainment, leading to a glut of down-to-earth books about thoughtful young heroines facing relatable school and family problems . . . and also a potentially murderous ghost. This shift began with the freaky supernatural work of Lois Duncan. She began her writing career in 1958 producing lighter teen fare, like the realistic *A Love Song for Joyce*. But her 1966 thriller *Ransom*, about a group of teens being held hostage on a school bus, changed the game. Initially rejected

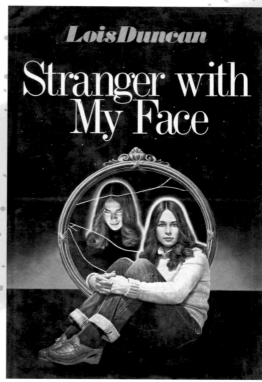

by her publisher for being too dark, the book was eventually published to great acclaim and nominated for an Edgar Award. In her 1971 family drama *A Gift of Magic*, she experimented with magical realism, and three years later Duncan truly broke ground on the mash-up of realist teen girl fiction and utterly bonkers supernatural stuff with her prep-school-possession novel *Down a Dark Hall*. For the rest of her career, Duncan peppered her suspense output with supernatural novels. Her 1976 book *Summer of Fear* tells the story of a woman who uses witchcraft to possess the body of a teen girl; 1981's *Stranger with My Face* is about one teen girl who uses astral projection to possess another girl's body.

Duncan was admittedly a pioneer of the supernatural subgenre, but other writers pioneered the angsty-girl-meets-ghost market. If you spent any time in elementary school looking askance at

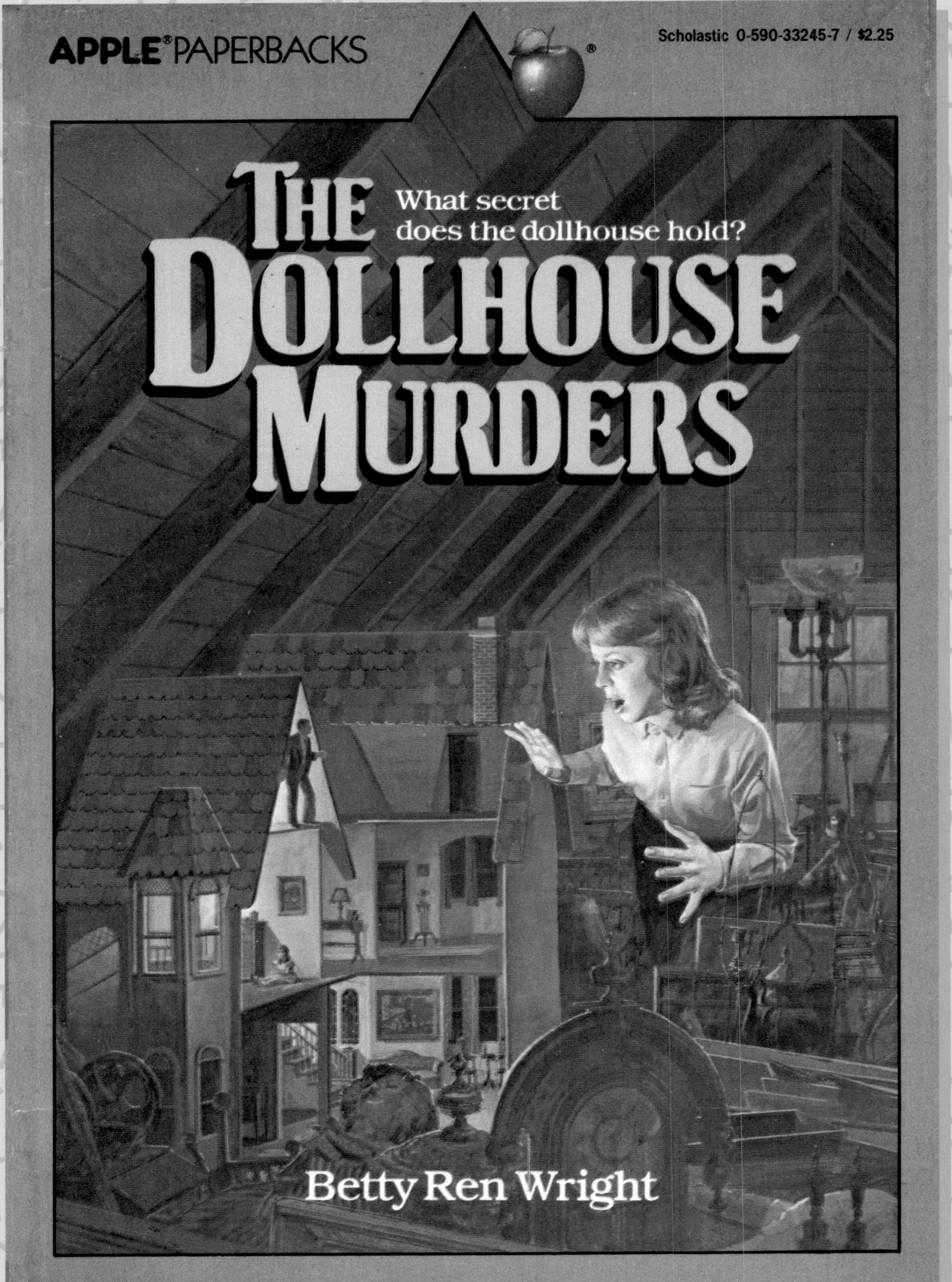
APPLE® PAPERBACKS
Scholastic 0-590-33245-7 / $2.25
THE DOLLHOUSE MURDERS
What secret does the dollhouse hold?
Betty Ren Wright

your (profoundly nonhaunted) dollhouse, you probably have Betty Ren Wright to thank. After decades of editing lighthearted and murder-free children's books, in her fifties Wright began writing the paranormal novels for which she's best known. And once she started, she became a one-woman microindustry. Her first spooky book was the 1982 psychic girl drama *The Secret Window*, which dedicated as much space to heroine Meg's friendship drama and parental divorce angst as it did to her struggles with prophetic dreams, thereby creating the blend of supernatural and family drama that would become Wright's hallmark.

Wright's follow-up the next year became her best-known work and first ghostly hit. *The Dollhouse Murders* set the standard for the era's ghost-meets-girl books with its spunky-yet-relatable female heroine dealing with family problems *and* benevolent spirits. After getting into a roaring fight with her parents over how much responsibility she needs to bear for her sister Louann, Amy moves in with her Aunt Clare. There, Amy finds a cool dollhouse modeled on the family home Clare lives in—and learns that her great-grandparents died in a gruesome double homicide and no one bothered to tell her. As one would expect, the dolls in the house begin reenacting the great-grandparents' murder and eventually help Amy solve the mystery of their deaths, neatly twining together the threads of family secret and ghostliness.

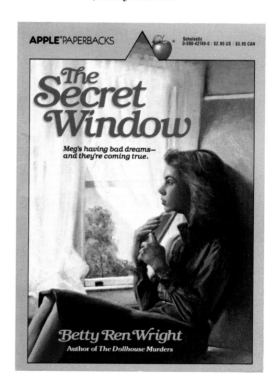

In 1984, Wright hammered home her role as *the* lady who wrote stories about sensitive tweens dealing with messes both familial and otherworldly with *Ghosts Beneath Our Feet*. This book covers a lot of the same ground as *Dollhouse*: Katie, her mother, and her stepbrother Jay are all spending the summer in their Uncle Frank's unexpectedly grim small hometown, to try to calm down after Jay's father's recent death. Of course, life in a depressed former mining town built atop the bodies of miners who died in an industrial accident thirty years earlier is not particularly calm. But it is full of family secrets that relate to a long-ago tragedy, encounters with an eerie female ghost who needs to give Katie a warning, and opportunities for a little personal growth.

Until her death in 2013, Wright committed consistently not just to scaring readers with her ghost stories, but also to normalizing the personal difficulties many kids struggle with. In fact, the most striking thing about these books might be how they gave girls' home life equal weight to their ghostly mysteries. Books like Wright's, or Sylvia Cassedy's 1983 novel *Behind the Attic Wall*, in which an antisocial and neglected orphan feels truly at peace only when she's chilling with haunted dolls, showed that dealing with ghosts is far from the most challenging thing going on in the heroines' lives—and, in fact, the dead often provide better emotional support than the living. Talking to spirits is easy; surviving an uncaring world and fractured family is the

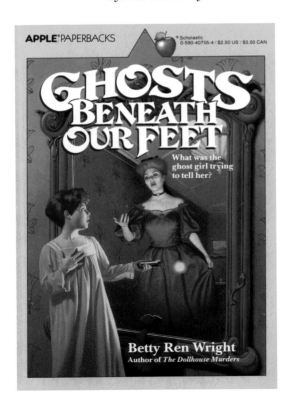

Molly Ringwald, is that you? In seriousness, if a book is about a spooky Victorian ghost, it's hard to resist portraying said ghost on the cover, puffed sleeves and all. But beyond fun outfits, putting the ghost smack on the front would help the young reader visualize a not-too-scary-and-blood-drippy image in their mind before reading.

truly supernatural feat.

Second only to Betty Ren Wright was middle grade ghost-lit queen Mary Dowling Hahn, and her 1986 novel *Wait Till Helen Comes* remains one of the most enduringly terrifying entries in the normal-girl-communes-with-undead-girl genre. Angry 7-year-old human Heather has been transplanted to the country to live with her dad and his new wife, so that they can become seminegligent artist parents to her and her new stepsiblings. Naturally, Heather quickly teams up with angry 7-year-old ghost Helen, because they have a lot in common: they're both simmering with rage, they both lost their mothers in tragic fires, and they both absolutely *hate* Heather's new family. Unfortunately, it soon becomes clear that Helen also hates the fact that Heather is alive. Unlike the helpful, guidance-counselor-style ghosts who populate the subgenre, Helen is vicious and terrifying and wants to drag Heather to the bottom of a nearby pond so she can play with her forever and ever. The book asks a heady question: what if even death doesn't offer refuge from the dumb mess of our lives? That's about as scary as a ghost trying to drag you to the bottom of a pond. (Fine, fine, the pond ghost is a *little* scarier.)

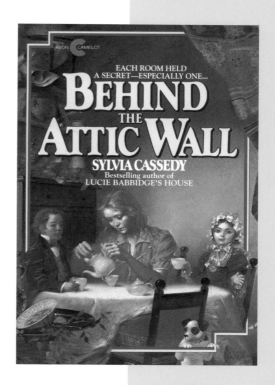

A similar philosophical thread winds through Jahnna N. Malcolm's 1991 middle grade novel *Scared Stiff*, a book about a group of hapless, bickering tweens who are stalked by—and eventually must fight—a reanimated corpse that runs around stabbing everyone. The kids use their ingenuity, compassion, and seventh-grade-level driving skills to evade certain death, but the book still closes on a nihilistic note: once the first corpse has been subdued, another reanimated body pops up, all without the kids ever understanding why corpses are rising in the first place, like a hellish *Groundhog Day*.

Some ghost stories for younger readers in the '80s and '90s were about a young woman gaining insight not into her family or the hellish world around her, but instead into how she doesn't need to ruin her life for some idiot boy. For example, Windswept was a series of romantic mysteries (mysterious romances?) put out by Scholastic between 1982 and 1984. A number of them married '80s romantic mystery with a progressive, feminist vibe, like Dorothy Francis's 1982 novel *The Ghost of Graydon Place*, which manages the trifecta of being a romantic mystery, maintaining a progressive feminist vibe, *and* being about ghosts. Only a cameo by Tiffany could make this book more '80s.

In *Graydon,* a group of wholesome teens (and one wholesome mom) are stranded during a snowstorm inside the titular Graydon Place, an abandoned mansion that is said to be haunted. And it is indeed haunted, by the surprisingly

APPLE PAPERBACKS

Scholastic
0-590-44996-6 / $2.75 US / $3.95 CAN

SCARED STIFF

Jahnna N. Malcolm

Somebody let
the body
out of the bag...

SCHOLASTIC

neurotic ghost of Victoria Graydon. Victoria doesn't seek to warn the heroes of impending danger, or to make them to choke to death on a corn dog so she'll have some company in the afterlife; she just wants to dish to innocent teen Tracy about her hundred-year-old romantic drama. "I know you're awake, Tracy. I can sense that you are. I can tell about things like that. Please talk to me. Please help me," Victoria moans in the night after entering Tracy's room uninvited, like an undead version of your most annoying college roommate.

We learn that Victoria's sister died suddenly after she stole Victoria's boyfriend. Victoria believes she killed her sister with her rage-thoughts, until Tracy discovers that in fact Victoria's crazy nanny killed the sister. But for Tracy, the real revelation is a personal one. A high school senior, she's been struggling with whether to pursue her dream of becoming a lawyer or to get married right after she graduates, which is what her idiot boyfriend Mac wants. Tracy realizes that, in addition to being a ghost, Victoria is kind of a loser who only talks or thinks about her (dead) boyfriend. This helps Tracy realize that she can put her dreams first, and if Mac doesn't like that, she knows a very nice dead girl she can set him up with.

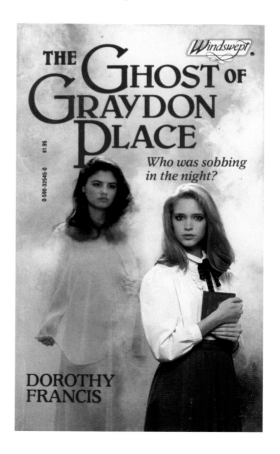

THE GHOST OF GRAYDON PLACE

Windswept

$1.95

0-590-32545-0

Who was sobbing in the night?

DOROTHY FRANCIS

How to Kill Friends and Incinerate People

Friendship is hard. If it wasn't, we wouldn't need to rely on social media to ensure that we never interact in meaningful ways with our friends. But for teens, the stakes are higher, the emotions more intense, and a minor betrayal can feel like the end of the world. And for fictional teens in the '80s and '90s . . . well, their angsty interpersonal drama often came with a body count. Unlike in the horror movies of the time, in which the killer was usually an adult, characters in YA horror novels often found themselves under attack by a deranged murderer who was also their peer.

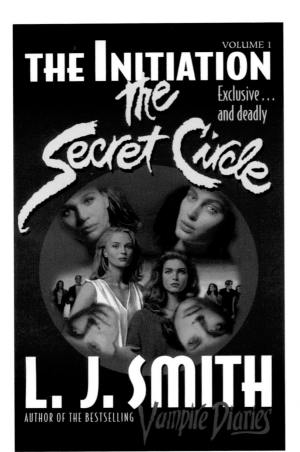

Sometimes, the situation was fairly straightforward. L. J. Smith's Secret Circle series, which debuted in 1992, chronicles all the ways teen witches can turn on each other, and Barbara Steiner's 1996 novel *Spring Break* asks who hasn't contemplated murdering their friends while on a long weekend away.

But other books took a more complicated approach to horror-friendship hybrids. As we've established, in the world of the '80s and '90s youth literature, you could not throw a sharpened machete without hitting a group of tweens forming a club, and horror fiction was no exception—especially in the books of one R. L. Stine. Stine started his writing career in the '70s, writing children's joke books under the name Jovial Bob Stine and publishing the Scholastic teen humor periodical *Bananas* (he somewhat mournfully told the *A.V. Club* in 2013, "I never wanted to be scary. I always wanted to be funny."). After some early '80s output that included books like *Indiana Jones and the Curse of Horror Island* and *The Siege of the Dragonriders*, Stine hit pay dirt with 1989's *The Babysitter*.

But what made Stine a household name was the Fear Street series, which debuted in 1989. Beginning with *The New Girl*, the books chronicled the lives of unlucky teens living in Shadyside, Ohio, whose moronic parents decided to raise them on the most evil, haunted, murder-ific street in America. The first few volumes quickly caught on, creating a bona fide phenomenon that rolled on for a full decade and included stories about prom queens, knives, and literally everything in between. So by 1994, it was about time the series turned its attention to the club trend, in book #24: *The Thrill Club*.

The Thrill Club is a group of teens who meet regularly to tell scary stories, and they are quite different from a certain group of Canadian teens who began gathering to exchange tales of terror in 1990, because in the Thrill Club, protagonist Talia's tales of throat-slashing terror feature her

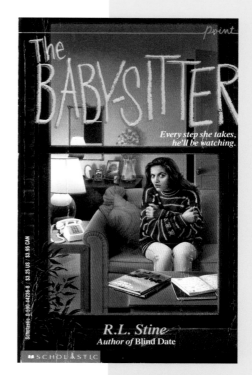

As R. L. Stine became the go-to guy for all things terror, his name got bumped up the visual hierarchy so that readers could identify and grab his titles with spine-chilling ease.

friends as characters. What could go wrong?! Of course, these friends start being murdered in real life, of course Talia is framed for it, and of course the boyfriend did it. (Plot twist: he did it by inhabiting Talia's body via some culturally insensitive "foreign" magic!)

Released in the same year, *The Thrill Club* and Christopher Pike's *The Midnight Club* might look like birds of a feather, based on their covers and back cover copy ("They were all going to die," reads Pike's book). But rather than the scary-story-club-gone-murderous promised on the cover, *Midnight Club* is in fact an extremely sensitive story of a group of teens living in hospice who gather regularly to tell spooky stories as an outlet for their fear and grief

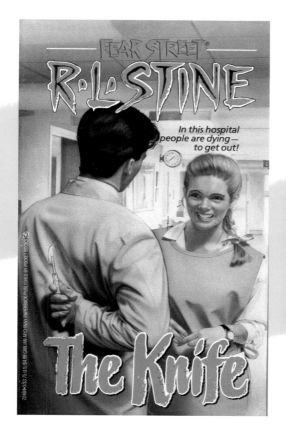

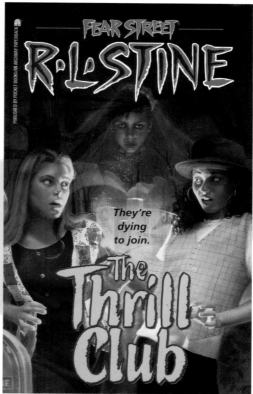

about impending death. And there's plenty of action: one character thinks she has gone into remission, then learns she was wrong; one character does kill another, in a death-with-dignity pact; and the club's stories themselves, presented in their entirety in the text, often feel like micro-Pike novels. This is a great piece of teen illness literature, more thoughtful in its examinations of what it means to be sick or to die than anything that came out of Lurlene McDaniel's word processor (see page 195).

Pike's career began in 1985 with the straightforward horror novel *Slumber Party*—a tale of revenge, spooky ski chalets, and blatant disregard for fire safety protocol—and he still produced plenty of meat-and-potatoes sci-fi and horror throughout the years, like 1991's *Die Softly* (see page 212) and 1992's *The Eternal Enemy*. But

As with R. L. Stine, Christopher Pike became a household name for teen and tween horror fans, getting an iconic type treatment for the covers of his novels.

Bestselling Author of Monster

Christopher Pike

The Eternal Enemy

Someone had come for her....

Author of The Last Vampire 3: Red Dice

Christopher Pike

The Midnight Club

Their stories became their lives. . . .

as his career progressed, more of his novels were concerned with spiritual matters, such as in *Midnight Club*, where the only "horror" is the chance that the characters might leave this world without learning the lessons they were fated to learn. That's why they gave it a misleading cover in order to sell it to eighth-graders!

While a lot of the era's horror existed in a bubble, shunning all social issues that were not psychotic stalkers, *Midnight Club* connects to the real world via an issue usually sidestepped in the subgenre. Club member Spence has been telling his friends that he has brain cancer and a girlfriend, but in reality, he's gay, dying of AIDS, and wracked with guilt over the possibility that he may have passed the disease on to his boyfriend, who is now dead from it. Spence's raw honesty about both his disease and the vicious peers whose behavior led him to stay closeted ("You can admit being gay if you're famous or live in the right part of the country, or even if you're older," he says. "But when you're a teenager, you have to hide and don't try to tell me that you don't.") is beyond striking for a book published in 1994. This didn't mean the book was well received by adults—*Publishers Weekly* described it as "A queasy blend of grisliness and New Age unctuousness"—but considering that it was published at the height of AIDS hysteria and at a time when unenlightened books about the disease like *It Happened to Nancy* were hitting store shelves, it's pretty damned groundbreaking.

A less groundbreaking flavor of friendship horror was the sorority horror novel. Sorority horror became a cinematic subgenre with 1974's *Black Christmas* (well, as "cinematic" as a movie that features a unicorn-figurine-based murder can be) that then blossomed in the '80s, with films including the Linda Blair vehicle *Hell Night* (1981), *The House on Sorority Row* (1984), *The Initiation* (1984), and *Sorority House Massacre* (1986). And, not surprisingly, we have our boy R. L. Stine to thank for sorority horror crossing over into YA. His 1987 book *Twisted* focuses on two sorority girls and one deranged sociopath . . . so, three sorority girls! A group of pledges

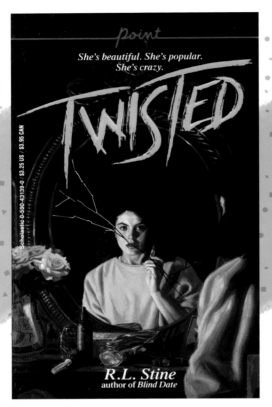

The cover of *Nightmare Hall* presents a twisted (get it?) take on the traditional, Sweet Valley–esque covers. Instead of an oval inset, there's a shadowy window, and while the type is pink, it's also set in a decidedly slasher-y font.

are taken out to the woods for a nice brutal hazing by their cruel tormentor, sorority sister Andrea. Andrea takes them through the paces of every sorority horror cliché, playing a prank that goes horribly wrong and thus creating a terrible secret that they all must keep forever. Would you be surprised to learn that this leads one of the pledges to have a psychotic break? What if I told you that she then covered her face in lipstick à la Diane Ladd in *Wild at Heart* and then tried to kill her fellow students? Would you be even more surprised if I told you that this psychotic break was actually caused by some stupid break-up with an idiot boyfriend? Of course you wouldn't be. This is R. L.'s world; we just make out with our dead, hunky ex-boyfriends and have psychotic breaks in it.

Deranged sorority princesses also showed up in Diane Hoh's Nightmare Hall, a twenty-nine-volume horror series that, from 1993 to 1995, took what I call "the Fear Street conundrum" to the next level. Moving away from a specific street is fairly easy, so long as you can find a buyer, but it'd be infinitely easier to leave Salem University, Nightmare Hall's deadly, ghost-filled murder college. I mean, I almost dropped out of college because I got bored reading *Moby-Dick*! These tormented teens need to stop toking up and fill out a friggin' transfer application!

Anyway, because Salem University is hell on earth, of course it has a robust Greek life. And in book #10, 1994's *Sorority Sister*, we learn that pledging a sorority doesn't only involve gaining access to as much jungle juice as you can chug; it also means being targeted by deranged sorority sister Candie, who is determined to destroy the sorority that her mom loves more than her, through such means as poisoned food, threatening hairdressers, and eventually bombs. Oh, and ants. She dumps a lot of ants in the sorority house, which as far as I know *is* a new one in teen horror. College students! Always innovating!

> **66 Everybody jumped on the bandwagon once they realized how popular it was. So at one point, it was just flooded and I do think that for a while it kind of died out, because I think that happens in publishing, you get a glut of a certain kind of book and then it's like overkill and then it kind of goes away for a while. 99**
>
> —RICHIE TANKERLSEY CUSICK, author of *The Mall* and *The Lifeguard*

A Conversation with Christopher Pike

For many readers, Christopher Pike needs no introduction. The author of best-selling teen thrillers like *Remember Me* and *The Last Vampire*, Pike (the pen name of author Kevin McFadden) is widely credited as having kick-started the YA horror trend with his 1985 book *Slumber Party*. I spoke to him about his thirty-plus-year career and the beginning of horror in YA.

ON *SLUMBER PARTY*:

"I wrote *Slumber Party* in what might be called a last-ditch effort to publish a book. By the time I sold it, I'd been writing non-stop every night, after work, for six years and I'd collected hundreds of rejection slips. . . . I tried my hand at a dozen different stories, primarily sci-fi novels. . . . I wasn't writing YA at the start of my career. Indeed, I knew little about the genre. I'd read *The Outsiders* and that was about it.

"But it was like there was some kind of steel wall around those New York publishers—there seemed no way to break through. Then my agent told me about a publishing house that was looking for YA thrillers. . . . He asked me if I could write a book for teens, a short novel around forty to fifty thousand words. I said sure and wrote *Slumber Party*. The original house I

wrote it for—the one who was starting a teen thriller series—rejected *Slumber Party* because, they said, it was too good. Now, maybe they were just trying kindly to brush me off, but my agent swore they were serious. Apparently, the editor thought the book should be treated with more respect and he didn't want it [as] his quickie series. Who knows? I am glad it ended up at Scholastic.

"It was originally a supernatural tale. When Jean Feiwel, who was at Avon at the time, first read it, she asked me to take out the supernatural elements. I said sure; I would have rewritten *Slumber Party* from the first to last page and have had it take place on the moon if Jean Feiwel was willing to publish it.

"I think *Slumber Party* became a popular book because it had a good story and was easy to read. That may sound like a simplistic answer but it is, in my opinion, accurate. . . . I was fortunate to show up at the right time. To be frank, I didn't have much competition, which, I know, may sound arrogant—although I'm actually trying to say I wasn't that special a novelist.

"I was no expert on the YA genre but I did my research. Once I'd sold my first book, I quickly read over a hundred YA novels and discovered that the authors were either treating their readers like they were awfully young or just plain stupid. Right from the start, I decided I wouldn't talk down to my readers. I'd write my YA books the same way I was writing my adult books—only the characters would be younger."

ON *THE LAST VAMPIRE* AND SPIRITUALITY IN HIS NOVELS:

"I was lucky *Slumber Party, Weekend,* and *Chain Letter* got on various best-seller lists, and Simon & Schuster came knocking. The head of the YA department, Pat MacDonald, told me they wanted to build my career—and after so many years of rejection, you can imagine how excited I was. Just as important, Pat said I could write whatever I wanted, which again was music to my ears. It was then I began to explore more exotic ideas. When I decided to write a vampire story with Sita as my heroine [*The Last Vampire*], I wanted to make her unlike any vampire that had ever been created. That's where her mystical element came from—sort of. In one sense, it was a calculated decision on my part to add such elements. However, writing from Sita's point of view was a classic example of how a character can take over a book. Sita began to do and say things I never imagined, and if you think maybe I channeled the book, I wouldn't argue with you. The bottom line is in all my later YA novels, I was trying to introduce new and wild and crazy ideas to the youth of America. And I like to think I succeeded at that."

ON HIS FANS:

"I have trouble believing [the fan mail I receive is] for me. It helps that my fans usually address their emails and letters to Christopher Pike and not Kevin McFadden. Somehow, in my twisted brain I'm able to think of Pike as someone unconnected to Kevin. This isn't me trying to be so humble or so politically correct. . . . To be blunt, I prefer to think of myself as a hack writer who just got lucky.

"When [*The Midnight Club*] came out, I received an avalanche of mail from teens who were dying, and from their parents, telling me how much the book meant to them; how it helped them face what was happening in their lives. I still get emails on that book; even more on *Remember Me* and the Last Vampire/Thirst series. . . . It's hard—no, impossible—to imagine that some weird story I dreamed up could help some stranger with such painful issues.

"And yet . . . there were a handful of books I read as a teen that changed my life. In seventh grade, I stumbled upon Arthur C. Clarke's *Childhood's End*. . . . I clearly remember how that book took me out of my life and transported me to a realm where anything was possible. That book had magic, it had fairy dust pressed between the pages. It had a power that changed my life, and it was that book that planted the seed of the dream that eventually became my life. What was that seed? It's simple—his novel inspired me to ask myself a question: "What if I could write such a book?""

I Always Feel Like Somebody's Watching Me

Love and romance are such core parts of adolescence that no story about teens is complete without them, even if said teens are busy running from a guy with a machete. That's how we got the YA horror novels of the '80s and '90s, which almost always seem to include a plot thread about dating, even if the protagonists should really be focused on not getting ax-murdered by the local ax murderer. Further complicating the situation is the fact that, in many of these novels, love itself was the horror. Such stories tended to fall into one of two camps: you just found out that your sweetie is a vampire/werewolf/chupacabra/surprisingly sexy kraken, or you're actually being stalked. Both are disappointing ways for a

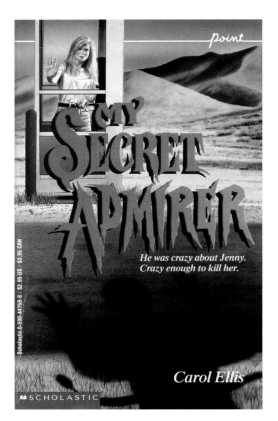

study hall flirtation to end. Stalking fever had infiltrated more realistic novels of the era (see page 178) fairly early on, but horror stalking novels hit their stride later in the '80s. And though these books shared the subject matter of some problem novels, horror stalking novels eschew the trauma and psychology and turn up the campiness. The villains resemble headline-grabbing criminals enough to satisfy readers' interest but remain absurd enough not to appear like real threats.

Carol Ellis didn't invent the horror stalker teen novel, but she did publish them early and often. *My Secret Admirer* (getting stalked while your parents are out of town) came out in

1989, *Silent Witness* (getting stalked because you know a terrible secret) in 1994, and *The Stalker* (getting stalked because you're in the touring cast of *Grease*) followed in 1996. *My Secret Admirer* is a classic example of the genre's cartoonishness; in it, a cute rich girl is basically abandoned by her negligent parents and then gets menaced in various ways by two creepy men. But it turns out that only one of the men is truly bad, and the other one (who seemed like a suspect 30 seconds ago!) is great now?

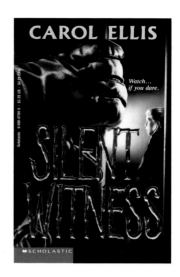

Unlike more realistic stalking books, these novels didn't focus on victim advocacy. Rather, they usually advocated for getting a boyfriend so that you'd have company the next time a stalker sees your parents are away for the weekend. Richie Tankersley Cusick's 1992 novel *The Mall* tracks shopping center employee Trish as she is stalked through the spooky corridors and deserted food courts, while her concerns about the weird guy menacing her are blown off by friends and police alike. Trish eventually helps take her stalker down, which might help explain the genre's popularity—heroines often triumphed over their stalkers in the end, a satisfaction sadly absent in most real-life cases.

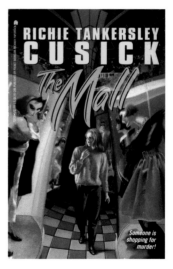

The teen stalking novels of R. L. Stine, however, take this genre to some thrillingly bizarre places. Though Stine's books cataloged pretty much every awful thing that could happen to a minor—from teen manslaughter and amnesia in his 1986 horror debut *Blind Date*, to killers who lust for babysitter blood in his 1989 breakthrough *The Babysitter*—Stine always seemed to have a real soft spot for stalker thrillers. The protagonists of his 1990 novel *The Boyfriend* live

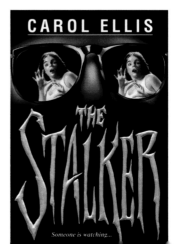

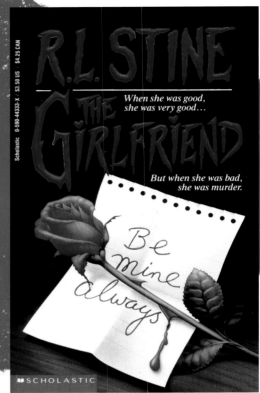

in a world of rich sensory details: Ralph Lauren sweaters! BMWs! Gloria Estefan songs! A movie that is for some reason described as an "action comedy with Robert De Niro grinning and shooting a lot of people and then driving a pick-up truck the wrong way on a freeway with a dozen police cars chasing him"! Heroine Joanne is a shallow-to-the-point-of-sociopathy spoiled rich jerk who kind of causes her boyfriend's death and then kind of doesn't care, because now she can spend more time with the guy she was cheating on her boyfriend with. Then her dead boyfriend appears to have come back as a zombie, but she doesn't notice for an extremely long time, because she is now too busy cheating on her new boyfriend with her old, dead(ish?) boyfriend. But *is* he a zombie? Or is Joanne just so mean and obsessed with high-end malls that she never even bothered to learn that zombies aren't real? I won't spoil that reveal for you, but suffice it to say that a major plot point hinges on someone leaving a door open because they assumed a maid would close it for them.

A year later, Stine followed up with the quasi sequel *The Girlfriend*, which features a male character getting more straightforwardly stalked by a female character but, sadly, no fake or real zombies. (There is a twist you might see coming if you read *The Babysitter*.) In both books, the victims seem less vulnerable and scared than those in stalking books by other authors—hell, in *The Boyfriend*, Joanne ultimately turns out to be the villain. Is this a lack of empathy on Stine's part? Or is his portrayal of stalking victims as not completely at their stalkers' mercy somehow progressive? In 1993, Stine turned out a more traditional stalker tale, *The Dead Girlfriend*, in which cute Annie is being antagonized by psycho Dawn, who is willing to stalk and murder anyone in order to get the Luke Perry–lookin' Jonathan all for herself. So really, the lesson is: in the world of Robert Lawrence Stine, chaos reigns.

❝ A lot of these books have problematic portrayals of women and dating. The main character's best friend is often overweight and interested in boys, and she's labeled (often, by the narrator) as boy-crazy, and therefore bad. There's also the issue of the 'Terrible Red Herring,' a love interest who turns out to be (whew!) not the killer. Oh, he stalked you for weeks and trapped you in his workout room and showed up in the backseat of your car, but he didn't actually kill anybody so you should totally be with him! ❞

—KELLY NUGENT and LINDSAY KATAI, comedians and hosts of teen horror novel podcast *Teen Creeps*

She loves him. She loves him. NOT.

I'd Love to Take You to the Prom, But I'm Dead

Of course, not every relationship in YA horror was terrible and defined by stalking. Some were even good relationships—so long as at least one party wasn't human. Human-monster romances have been a staple of supernatural literature since at least the nineteenth century, when formative vampire stories *The Vampyre* (1818) and *Carmilla* (1871) pioneered the concept of the beautiful, seductive vampire who wants more from humans than their blood, if you get my drift. But in '80s horror YA, human-meets-ghoul love stories proliferated. Perhaps it was because, with the AIDS epidemic reshaping how we dated and mated, sex felt scary. Perhaps

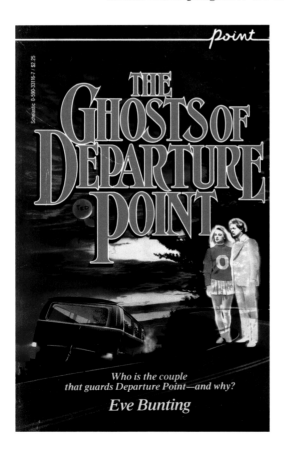

Who is the couple that guards Departure Point—and why?

Eve Bunting

it was the fault of the 1976 best seller *Interview with the Vampire*, which brought sexy vampires into the public consciousness. Perhaps it was Nancy Reagan's inspiring and high-profile relationship with an evil, haunted ventriloquist's dummy. Whatever the cause, by the mid-'80s, human teens simply could not get enough of the sex lives of monsters.

Eve Bunting's 1982 book *The Ghosts of Departure Point*, features a meet-cute between teens Vicki and Ted who realize they are both ghosts who are cursed to haunt Departure Point for causing auto accidents that ended in multiple deaths, including their own. Adorbs! They then fall in love, their joy sullied only by the fact that they've been cursed to Departure

Point not to suck undead face, but to prevent future auto accidents. But if they succeed in preventing people from dying in car wrecks, they'll get ferried off to the afterlife, where who knows what the rules about face-sucking are! Eventually, Ted and Vicki decide to fix Departure Point by scaring the townspeople into repairing the road. (Why the townspeople find the idea of ghosts scarier than tons of people dying on this road is hard to say.) As a reward, Ted and Vicki get to come back to life, now slightly wiser about auto safety.

Bunting seems to have been hung up on amorous ghosts, because in 1984 she was back on the case with her book *Ghost Behind Me*, which promises human-on-spectre action with its sexy tagline: "The Ghost is pulling her into his past . . . can she resist his dark allure?" We learn that she very much can. Sure, Felix the ghost is pretty hunky for a dead person, but the way he follows young Cinnamon around her new family home and neighborhood is creepy. (Wait, is this book a combination of sexy monster novel and stalking novel? Or is it just presaging Twilight?). In fact, he's just trying to connect with the spirit of his dead girlfriend. Ugh, you know guys trapped between the worlds of the living and the dead: never able to commit.

By the '90s, America had decided that those nineteenth-century writers were on to something; ghosts were out, and vampires were sexual napalm. Years before the TV debut of *Buffy the Vampire Slayer*, YA readers

GHOST BEHIND ME

The Ghost is pulling her into his past . . . can she resist his dark allure?

EVE BUNTING

BC 62211-0/$2.50/PUBLISHED BY POCKET BOOKS/AN ARCHWAY PAPERBACK

Author of <u>The Midnight Club</u> and <u>The Wicked Heart</u>

Christopher PiKE

This time someone is hunting her . . . .

$3.99 U.S./$5.99 CAN /AN ARCHWAY PAPERBACK PUBLISHED BY POCKET BOOKS

The Last Vampire

Christopher Pike's take on vamps stuck with the visual branding of his other titles (see page 228), ditching the expected reds and blacks for a peppy pink and zippy yellow.

were gifted a number of books about sexy teen vampires and the humans who hope to take them to homecoming, including L. J. Smith's Vampire Diaries series in 1991; Christopher Pike's Last Vampire series in 1994, and Janice Harrell's Vampire's Love series in 1995. (The Vampire Diaries novels continued to be published until 2014, but due to a strange contract situation, L. J. Smith was fired from writing the books in 2011 and began publishing her own volumes in 2014 as fan fiction.)

Although we now think of vampiric love as a match between a moody male immortal and a pretty human high school girl who just wants to soothe him, Pike and Harrell's books turned that dynamic on its head with powerful female vampires hitting on boys several hundreds to thousand years their junior. In Pike's *The Last Vampire*, which started the series, a high-school vampire named Alisa reveals that not only is she being hunted by the *last* vampire, but she's actually a 5,000-year-old woman named Sita who was sired by the very *first* vampire. While trying to figure out what to do about her hunter and casually killing anyone who runs afoul of her, Alisa/Sita meets and falls for Ray, a local high school boy, and this is really the biggest twist of all: that a woman who has been alive for millennia wants to hang around an adolescent male.

A version of the same situation runs through Harrell's *Vampire's Love, Volume I: Blood Curse*, wherein Rina—the titular blood-cursin' vampire who is hot, horny, and eternally 16—gets stuck on the notably average James, who she thinks looks like "some spectral

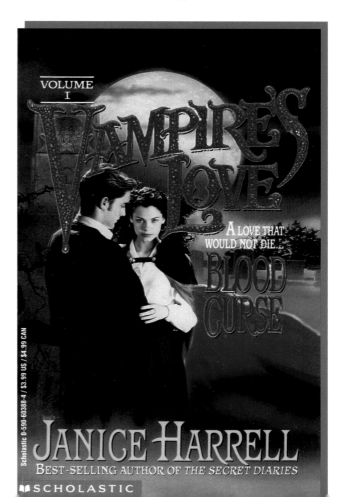

prince come to take her to the underworld" (*okay*, then). Like Stephenie Meyer's Edward Cullen, Rina is fine with just sneaking into a house and watching her honey sleep whenever the mood strikes. But unlike Edward Cullen, Rina has bona fides: she's from Transylvania, she can turn into a bat, and she has a cape, just like a legit vampire. She also murders any sassy juvenile delinquents who get in her way, and she sorta kinda accidentally turns James's annoying girlfriend into a vampire (oopsy!), who then turns other kids at school into members of a sort of vampire bully clique (double oopsy!). Given that *Twilight* rode to the top by positing that a vampire is basically the ultimate sophisticated older boyfriend (take that, dudes with mopeds!), it's interesting that so many of these earlier books present the inverse fantasy, that the cool vampire girlfriend would do her damnedest to protect her human beau using her wisdom, life experience, and affinity for murder.

If you're still not convinced that '90s America was wild for the idea of sexual congress with a monster, consider Sweet Valley High's werewolf books. This series had, of course, been all about over-the-top plotlines since day one, but a hulking new level of implausibility clawed its way into SVH #104: *Love and Death in London* in 1994. (It's weird that the title doesn't mention anything about a werewolf, right? Especially when you consider that the other titles in this plot arc are *A Date with a Werewolf* and *Beware the Wolfman*.) The twins travel to London for internships, and they land just as the area is rocked by a series of murders that seem to have been committed by . . . . a wolf. But where do you find a wolf in modern-day London? In Elizabeth's boudoir, perhaps? (Hint: check your local royal family for secret illegitimate children who have gone mad with rage and possibly suffer from lycanthropy.)

Despite the suggestion that the perfect-size-6 Cali princesses might be torn limb from limb by a man-beast (finally!), the whole werewolf arc doesn't feel terribly different in execution from the Wakefields' past high-drama antics. Hey, some days you date a werewolf, and others you get your sister drunk so you can beat her for the title of prom queen and then she gets in a car crash that kills your boyfriend! Forget about it, Jessica, it's Sweet Valleytown! More than anything, the SVH wolf-man arc is a tribute to how omnipresent and powerful YA horror was in '90s—even stalwarts as peachy-keen as Sweet Valley High wanted in on the dark, brooding action.

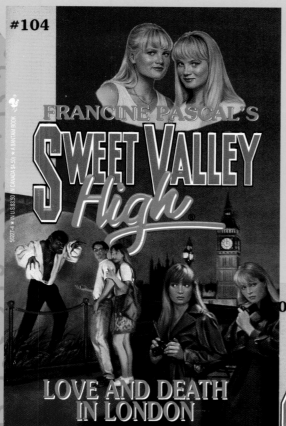

#104

FRANCINE PASCAL'S

SWEET VALLEY
High ®

LOVE AND DEATH
IN LONDON

05

FRANCINE PASCAL'S

SWEET VALLEY
High ®

PRINCESS
ELIANA
MURDER
VICTIM
?

A DATE WITH
A WEREWOLF

NOW A
HIT TV
SERIES!

Extra Credit Reading

Though researching this book was primarily a matter of calling out sick from work so that I could read *The Dollhouse Murders*, a number of texts about young adult and middle grade literature proved immeasurably helpful. Whether they placed the books I was reading in a larger historical context, illuminated issues the YA publishing industry has been grappling with for decades, or simply revealed how your teen book sausage gets made, I couldn't have written *Paperback Crush* without them.

Boesky, Amy. "The Ghost Writes Back." *Kenyon Review Online*, Winter 2013. https://www.kenyonreview.org/kr-online-issue/2013-winter/selections/amy-boesky-656342.

Boyes, Kathleen. "The Queen of Teen Romance: How Francine Pascal Built an Empire Without Writing a Single 'Sweet Valley' Book." *Chicago Tribune*, October 2, 1991.

Carpan, Carolyn. *Sisters, Schoolgirls and Sleuths: Girls' Series Books in America.* Lanham, MD: The Scarecrow Press, 2009.

Cart, Michael. *From Romance to Realism: 50 Years of Growth and Change in Young Adult Literature.* New York: HarperCollins, 1996.

Hinton, S. E. "Teen-Agers Are for Real." *New York Times*, August 27, 1967.

Larrick, Nancy. "The All-White World of Children's Books." *Saturday Review*, September 11, 1965.

Marcus, Leonard S., ed. *Dear Genius: The Letters of Ursula Nordstrom.* New York: HarperCollins, 1998.

Pattee, Amy. *Reading the Adolescent Romance: Sweet Valley High and the Popular Young Adult Romance Novel.* New York: Routledge, 2011.

Swerdloff, Alexis. "Ann M. Martin on the Enduring Appeal of *The Baby-Sitters Club* and Rebooting Another Children's Series." Vulture.com, September 5, 2016. http://www.vulture.com/2016/09/ann-m-martin-missy-piggle-wiggle.html.

Credits

Listed below is publisher and cover artist information for each book reproduced in *Paperback Crush*. We have tried to include complete and accurate names, titles, and dates. Please contact the publisher to correct omissions or errors in attribution. All artwork copyright of the artists.

PAGE 14: *Couples: Changing Partners* by M. E. Cooper (Scholastic, 1986), cover artist unknown. **PAGE 17:** *Sixteen Can Be Sweet* by Maud Johnson (Scholastic, 1978), cover artist unknown. **PAGE 18:** *Love Comes to Anne* by Lucille S. Warner (Scholastic, 1979), cover artist unknown. **PAGE 19:** *Just the Way You Are* by Janice Boies (Bantam, 1986), cover photo by Pat Hill. *Promise Me Love* by Jane Redish (Bantam, 1986), cover photo by Pat Hill. *The Other Me* by Terri Fields (Bantam, 1986), cover photo by Pat Hill. **PAGE 20:** *Sunfire: Amanda* by Candice F. Ransom (Scholastic, 1984), cover artist unknown. *Wishing Star: The Lost Summer* by Joan Oppenheimer (Scholastic, 1977), cover photo by Owen Brown. **PAGE 21:** *Couples: Making Promises* by M. E. Cooper (Scholastic, 1986), cover artist unknown. *Sing About Us* by Winifred Madison (Scholastic, 1982), cover photo by Owen Brown. **PAGE 22:** *Nice Girls Don't* by Caroline Cooney (Scholastic, 1984), cover artist unknown. *The Boy Barrier* by Jesse DuKore (Scholastic, 1985), cover artist unknown. **PAGE 26:** *Megan the Klutz* by Alida Young (Willowisp, 1986), cover artist unknown. **PAGE 27:** *How I Broke Up with Ernie* by R. L. Stine (Story House Corp, 1990), cover artist unknown. *The Plot against the Pom-Pom Queen* by Ellen Leroe (Berkley, 1985), cover artist unknown. **PAGE 28:** *If This Is Love, I'll Take Spaghetti* by Ellen Conford (Scholastic, 1983), cover artist unknown. *Karen Kepplewhite Is the World's Best Kisser* by Eve Bunting (Clarion, 1982), cover artist unknown. **PAGE 30:** *Finding My Voice* by Marie G. Lee (Laurel Leaf, 1992), cover artist unknown. *I'll Get There, It Better Be Worth The Trip* by John Donovan (Harper & Row, 1969), cover artist unknown. **PAGE 31:** *Happy Endings Are All Alike* by Sandra Scoppettone (Laurel Leaf, 1978), cover artist unknown. **PAGE 32:** *Annie on My Mind* by Nancy Garden (Farrar, Straus and Giroux, 1982), cover artist unknown. *Ruby* by Rosa Guy (Penguin, 1976), cover artist unknown. **PAGE 34:** *Caitlin: The Promises Trilogy #2: Promises Broken* by Francine Pascal (Bantam, 1986), cover art by Bantam Books Inc. **PAGE 35:** *Caitlin: The Love Trilogy #3: True Love* by Francine Pascal (Bantam, 1986), cover photo by Mark Witz. **PAGE 37:** *Dream Your Own Romance #2: Holiday Romance* by Julie Cahn (Simon & Schuster, 1983), cover artist unknown. **PAGE 38:** *Make Your Dreams Come True #3: Worthy Opponents* by Nicole Carr (Warner, 1984), cover photo by Bill Cadge, cover design by Gene Light. **PAGE 39:** *Changing Places* by Susan Smith (Scholastic, 1986), cover artist unknown. **PAGE 40:** *Phone Calls* by R. L. Stine (Archway, 1990), cover art by Mike Wimmer. **PAGE 42:** *Forever . . .* by Judy Blume (Pocket, 1975), cover artist unknown. **PAGE 43:** *Up in Seth's Room* by Norma Fox Mazer (Laurel Leaf, 1979), cover artist unknown. **PAGE 44:** *Sooner or Later* by Bruce Hart and Carol Hart (Avon, 1978), cover artist unknown. **PAGE 45:** *Waiting Games* by Bruce Hart and Carol Hart (Avon, 1981), cover artist unknown. **PAGE 46:** *Domestic Arrangements* by Norma Klein (Evans, 1981), cover artist unknown. **PAGE 50:** *We Hate Everything but Boys* by Linda Lewis (Archway, 1985), cover art by Richard Lauter. **PAGE 53:** *The Against Taffy Sinclair Club* by Betsy Haynes (Bantam, 1978), cover art by Bantam Books Inc. **PAGE 54:** *Taffy Sinclair Strikes Again* by Betsy Haynes (Bantam, 1984), cover art by Rich Williams. *Taffy Sinclair, Baby Ashley, and Me* by Betsy Haynes (Bantam, 1987), cover art by Lino Saffiotti. **PAGE 55:** *The Fabulous Five #18: Teen Taxi* by Betsy Haynes (Bantam, 1990), cover art by Andrew Bacha. *The Fabulous Five #24: The Great TV Turn-Off* by Betsy Haynes (Skylark, 1991), cover artist unknown. **PAGE 56:** *Preteen Means In Between* by Linda Lewis (Pocket, 1993), cover artist unknown. *2 Young 2 Go 4 Boys* by Linda Lewis (Archway, 1988), cover art by Charles Lilly. **PAGE 57:** *Friends 4-Ever #3: 2 Sweet 2 B 4-Gotten* by

Deidre Corey (Scholastic, 1990), cover artist unknown. *Friends 4-Ever #1: P.S. We'll Miss You* by Deidre Corey (Scholastic, 1990), cover artist unknown. **PAGE 58:** *Boy Talk: Sneaking Around* by Betsy Haynes (Random House, 1995), cover art by Aleta Jenks. *Swept Away 8: All Shook Up* by Eileen Goudge (Avon, 1987), cover artist unknown. **PAGE 60:** *Sleepover Friends #3: Kate's Surprise* by Susan Saunders (Scholastic, 1987), cover artist unknown. *Sleepover Friends #2: Starring Stephanie* by Susan Saunders (Scholastic, 1987), cover artist unknown. **PAGE 61:** *Sleepover Friends #13: Patti's Secret Wish* by Susan Saunders (Scholastic, 1989), cover artist unknown. **PAGE 62:** *Girl Talk #1: Welcome to Junior High* by L. E. Blair (Western Publishing, 1990), cover artist unknown. **PAGE 64:** *Sorority Sisters #1: For Members Only* by Marjorie Sharmat (Laurel Leaf, 1986), cover artist unknown. **PAGE 65:** *NEATE to the Rescue!* by Debbi Chocolate (Just Us Books, 1992), cover art by Melodye Rosales. **PAGE 67:** *NEATE: Elizabeth's Wish* by Debbi Chocolate (Just Us Books, 1994), cover artist unknown. *Kid Caramel, Private Investigator #3: Mess at Loch Ness* by Dwayne J. Ferguson (Just Us Books, 2003), cover artist unknown. **PAGE 68:** *I Want to Go Home!* by Gordon Korman (Apple, 1981), cover artist unknown. **PAGE 69:** *Bummer Summer* by Ann M. Martin (Scholastic, 1983), cover artist unknown. *Camp Sunnyside Friends #1: No Boys Allowed!* by Marilyn Kaye (Avon, 1989), cover artist unknown. **PAGE 71:** *Cheerleaders #2: Getting Even* by Christopher Pike (Scholastic, 1985), cover artist unknown. *The Gymnasts #7: Tumbling Ghosts* by Elizabeth Levy (Scholastic, 1989), cover artist unknown. **PAGE 72:** *Bad News Ballet #2: Battle of the Bunheads* by Jahnna N. Malcolm (Apple, 1989), cover artist unknown. **PAGE 73:** *The Saddle Club #8: Horse Show* by Bonnie Bryant (Bantam, 1989), cover artist unknown. **PAGE 75:** *Pony Pals: Keep Out, Pony!* by Jeanne Betancourt (Scholastic, 1996), cover artist unknown. *Pony Pals: The Winning Pony* by Jeanne Betancourt (Scholastic, 1999), cover artist unknown. **PAGE 76:** *The Pink Parrots #1: The Girls Strike Back* by Lucy Ellis (Little, Brown & Co., 1990), cover art by Jeff Mangiat. **PAGE 77:** *Girl Friends #1: Draw the Line* by Nicole

Grey (Kensington, 1993), cover artist unknown. **PAGE 78:** *18 Pine Street #1: Sort of Sisters* by Walter Dean Myers (Bantam, 1992), cover photo by Marc Witz. *18 Pine Street # 2: The Party* by Walter Dean Myers (Bantam, 1992), cover photo by Marc Witz. **PAGE 80:** *Going on Twelve* by Candice F. Ransom (Scholastic, 1988), cover artist unknown. *Dear Diary #1: The Party* by Carrie Randall (Apple, 1989), cover artist unknown. **PAGE 81:** *Best Friends #13: Who's Out to Get Linda?* by Susan Smith (Pocket, 1991), cover artist unknown. **PAGE 82:** *You've Been Away All Summer* by Sheila Hayes (Scholastic, 1986), cover artist unknown. *Invisible Lissa* by Natalie Honeycutt (Avon, 1985), cover artist unknown. **PAGE 84:** *The Summer of Mrs. MacGregor* by Betty Ren Wright (Scholastic, 1986), cover artist unknown. *If It Hadn't Been for Yoon Jun* by Marie G. Lee (Avon, 1993), cover artist unknown. **PAGE 85:** *You, Me, And Gracie Makes Three* by Dean Marney (Scholastic, 1989), cover artist unknown. **PAGE 87:** *Slam Book* by Ann M. Martin (Point, 1989), cover artist unknown. **PAGE 90:** *Sweet Valley High #38: Leaving Home* by Francine Pascal (Bantam, 1987), cover photo by Cloverdale Press. **PAGE 93:** *The Divorce Express* by Paula Danziger (Laurel Leaf, 1982), cover artist unknown. **PAGE 94:** *What's Best for You* by Judie Angell (Laurel Leaf, 1981), cover artist unknown. *Angel Face* by Norma Klein (Fawcett, 1984), cover artist unknown. **PAGE 95:** *The Great Male Conspiracy* by Betty Bates (Dell Yearling, 1986), cover artist unknown. *Boys Are Yucko!* by Anna Grossnickle Hines (Scholastic, 1989), cover artist unknown. **PAGE 96:** *Memo: To Myself When I Have a Teenage Kid* by Carol Snyder (Putnam, 1983), cover artist unknown. *The Facts and Fictions of Minna Pratt* by Patricia MacLachlan (Harper, 1988), cover artist unknown. **PAGE 97:** *Standing Ovation* by Audra Spotts (Tempo, 1983), cover artist unknown. *The Sunita Experiment* by Mitali Perkins (Scholastic, 1993), cover artist unknown. **PAGE 98:** *Good-Bye Pink Pig* by C. S. Adler (Avon, 1985), cover artist unknown. **PAGE 100:** *Tiger Eyes* by Judy Blume (Laurel Leaf, 1981), cover artist unknown. **PAGE 102:** *How to Talk to Boys and Other Important People* by Catherine Winters (Bantam, 1983), cover photo by Pat Hill. **PAGE 103:** *The Judy Blume Diary* by Judy Blume (Dell, 1981), cover artist unknown. *Sweet Valley Twins Super Summer Fun Book* by Laurie Pascal Wenk (Bantam, 1990), cover artist unknown. **PAGE 105:** *Sweet Valley High #82: Kidnapped by the Cult!* by Francine Pascal (Bantam, 1992), cover art by Daniel Weiss Associates Inc. **PAGE 106:** *Sweet Valley High #32: The New Jessica* by Francine Pascal (Bantam, 1986), cover art by Cloverdale Press. **PAGE 109:** *Red Hair* by Charlotte St. John (Fawcett, 1989), cover artist unknown. *Red Hair, Too* by Charlotte St. John (Fawcett, 1991), cover artist unknown. **PAGE 110:** *Three Sisters* by Norma Fox Mazer (Point, 1986), cover artist unknown. **PAGE 111:** *Cousins* by Virginia Hamilton (Apple, 1990), cover artist unknown. *Cousins #1: Not Quite Sisters* by Colleen O'Shaughnessy McKenna (Apple, 1993), cover artist unknown. **PAGE 112:** *Whitney Cousins: Erin* by Jean Thesman (Avon, 1990), cover artist unknown. *Whitney Cousins: Triple Trouble* by Jean Thesman (Avon, 1992), cover artist unknown. **PAGE 116:** *The Girls of Canby Hall #15: To Tell the Truth* by Emily Chase (Scholastic, 1986), cover artist unknown. **PAGE 119:** *Junior High: How Dumb Can You Get?* By Karen Kenyon (Scholastic, 1987), cover artist unknown. *Junior High: The Great Eighth Grade Switch* by Karen Kenyon (Scholastic, 1988), cover artist unknown. **PAGE 120:** *Class of '88: Junior* by Linda A. Cooney (Scholastic, 1987), cover artist unknown. *Video High #1: Modern Love* by Marilyn Kaye (Kensington, 1994), cover artist unknown. **PAGE 122:** *The B.Y. Times #3: Twins in Trouble* by Leah Klein (Targum Press, 1991), cover artist unknown. *Maudie and Me and the Dirty Book* by Betty Miles (Avon, 1980), cover art by Patricia Henderson Lincoln. **PAGE 124:** *Sixth Grade Can Really Kill You* by Barthe DeClements (Scholastic, 1985), cover artist unknown. *Our Sixth-Grade Sugar Babies* by Eve Bunting (HarperCollins, 1990), cover artist unknown. **PAGE 126:** *Trish for President* by Lael Littke (Archway, 1984), cover art by Steve Gross. **PAGE 127:** *Senior Year #1: Homecoming Dance* by Janet Quin-Harkin (Harper, 1991), cover art by Daniel Weiss Associates Inc. *Operation: Save the Teacher* by Meg Wolitzer (Avon, 1993), cover artist

unknown. **PAGE 129:** *Sex Education* by Jenny Davis (Laurel Leaf, 1988), cover artist unknown. **PAGE 130:** *Sex Education* by Jenny Davis (Laurel Leaf, 1995), cover artist unknown. **PAGE 132:** *The Girls of Canby Hall #18: Making Friends* by Emily Chase (Scholastic, 1986), cover artist unknown. **PAGE 133:** *Pen Pals #1: Boys Wanted!* by Sharon Dennis Wyeth (Dell Yearling, 1989), cover artist unknown. **PAGE 134:** *Campus Fever: Crash Course* by Joanna Wharton (Signet, 1985), cover artist unknown. *Sweet Valley University 1: College Girls* by Francine Pascal (Bantam, 1993), cover art by Daniel Weiss Associates Inc. **PAGE 135:** *Reality 101: Never Fall in Love* by Dahlia Kosinski (Harper, 1995), cover artist unknown. **PAGE 138:** *The Baby-Sitters Club #1: Kristy's Great Idea* by Ann M. Martin (Apple, 1986), cover art by Dale Dyer. **PAGE 141:** *Katie's Baby-Sitting Job* by Martha Tolles (Scholastic, 1985), cover artist unknown. **PAGE 142:** *Baby-Sitting Is a Dangerous Job* by Willo Davis Roberts (Fawcett, 1985), cover artist unknown. *Baby-Sitting for Fun and Profit* by Rubie Saunders (Archway, 1972), cover artist unknown. **PAGE 144:** *The Baby-Sitters Club #71: Claudia and the Perfect Boy* by Ann M. Martin (Apple, 1994), cover art by Hodges Soileau. *The Baby-Sitters Club #27: Jessi and the Superbrat* by Ann M. Martin (Apple, 1989), cover art by Hodges Soileau. *The Baby-Sitters Club #2: Claudia and the Phantom Phone Calls* by Ann M. Martin (Apple, 1986), cover art by Dale Dyer. **PAGE 145:** *The Baby-Sitters Club #34: Mary Anne & Too Many Boys* by Ann M. Martin (Apple, 1990), cover art by Hodges Soileau. *The Baby-Sitters Club #11: Kristy and the Snobs* by Ann M. Martin (Apple, 1989), cover art by Hodges Soileau *The Baby-Sitters Club #23: Dawn on the Coast* by Ann M. Martin (Apple, 1989), cover art by Hodges Soileau. *The Baby-Sitters Club #3: The Truth About Stacey* by Ann M. Martin (Apple, 1986), cover art by Hodges Soileau. **PAGE 147:** *Sunset Island* by Cherie Bennett (Berkley, 1991), cover art by General Licensing Company, Inc. *Samantha Slade: Monster Sitter #1* by Susan Smith (Archway, 1987), cover artist unknown. **PAGE 149:** *Baby-Sitters Club Friends Forever Special: Graduation Day* by Anne M. Martin (Scholastic, 2000), cover artist unknown. *The*

Baby-Sitters Club #88: Farewell, Dawn by Ann M. Martin (Scholastic, 1995), cover art by Hodges Soileau. **PAGE 150:** *@Cafe #2: I'll Have What He's Having* by Elizabeth Craft (Archway, 1997), cover art by Daniel Weiss Associates Inc. **PAGE 151:** *Heartbreak Cafe #6: Just Desserts* by Janet Quin-Harkin (Fawcett, 1990), cover artist unknown. *The Merivale Mall #2: The Best of Everything* by Jana Ellis (Troll, 1989), cover artist unknown. **PAGE 153:** *Girls R.U.L.E. #1: Girls to the Rescue* by Kris Lowe (Berkley, 1998), cover artist unknown. *Love and Betrayal and Hold the Mayo* by Francine Pascal (Laurel Leaf, 1985), cover artist unknown. **PAGE 154:** *Camp Girl-Meets-Boy* by Caroline Cooney (Bantam, 1988), cover art by Katherine Thompson. *Camp Reunion* by Caroline Cooney (Bantam, 1988), cover art by Ben Stahl. **PAGE 155:** *There's a Bat in Bunk Five* by Paula Danziger (Delacorte, 1980), cover artist unknown. **PAGE 156:** *Teen Angels #2: Love Never Dies* by Cherie Bennett (Avon, 1996), cover artist unknown. **PAGE 157:** *Med Center #1: Virus* by Diane Hoh (Scholastic, 1996), cover artist unknown. **PAGE 158:** *The Nancy Drew Files Case #58: Hot Pursuit* by Carolyn Keene (Archway, 1991), cover art by Tom Galasinski. **PAGE 159:** *Love Me Deadly* by Blossom Elfman (Fawcett, 1989), cover artist unknown. **PAGE 160:** *The Trouble with Lemons* by Daniel Hayes (Fawcett, 1991), cover artist unknown. *Tripper & Sam #2: Danger on the Sound Track* by Nancy K. Robinson (Scholastic, 1986), cover artist unknown. *The Case of the Frightened Rock Star* by Elizabeth Levy (Pocket, 1980), cover artist unknown. **PAGE 161:** *Shock Effect* by Glen Ebisch (Crosswinds, 1987), cover artist unknown. *Spy Girls: If Looks Could Kill* by Elizabeth Cage (Archway, 1999), cover art by 17th Street. **PAGE 162:** *All That Glitters #8: Award Night* by Kristi Andrews (Bantam, 1988), cover artist unknown. **PAGE 163:** *Stardust* by Alane Ferguson (Avon, 1993), cover artist unknown. **PAGE 164:** *Bewitched* by Isla Fisher (Penguin, 1995), cover artist unknown. **PAGE 166:** *Stay on Your Toes, Maggie Adams!* by Karen Strickler Dean (Avon, 1986), cover photo by Doyle Gray. *Wild Hearts Forever* by Cherie Bennett (Archway, 1994), cover artist un-

known. **PAGE 167:** *Anastasia's Chosen Career* by Lois Lowry (Dell Yearling, 1987), cover artist unknown. **PAGE 168:** *Dream Girls #1: Anything to Win!* by Rosemary Joyce (Archway, 1986), cover art by James Mathewuse. **PAGE 172:** *The Face on the Milk Carton* by Caroline Cooney (Bantam, 1990), cover art by Derek James. **PAGE 174:** The *Late Great Me* by Sandra Scoppettone (Bantam, 1976), cover artist unknown. *Steffie Can't Come Out to Play* by Fran Arrick (Laurel Leaf, 1978), cover artist unknown. *Don't Hurt Laurie!* by Willo Davis Roberts (Simon & Schuster, 1977), cover artist unknown. **PAGE 176:** *Twice Taken* by Susan Beth Pfeffer (Laurel Leaf, 1994), cover artist unknown. **PAGE 177:** *The Girl in the Box* by Ouida Sebestyen (Bantam, 1988), cover art by Derek James. **PAGE 178:** *Are You Alone in the House?* by Richard Peck (Laurel Leaf, 1976), cover artist unknown. **PAGE 179:** *Desperate Pursuit* by Gloria D. Miklowitz (Bantam, 1992), cover art by George Tsui. **PAGE 181:** *Connie* by John Benton (New Hope Books, 1982), cover artist unknown. **PAGE 182:** *Ask Me If I Care* by H. B. Gilmore (Fawcett, 1985), cover artist unknown. *Friends for Life* by Ellen Emerson White (Avon, 1983), cover artist unknown. **PAGE 183:** *Beauty Queen* by Linda Glovach (HarperCollins, 1998), cover artist unknown. **PAGE 185:** *Who Killed My Daughter?* by Lois Duncan (Dell, 1992), cover artist unknown. **PAGE 187:** *We All Fall Down* by Robert Cormier (Delacorte, 1991), cover artist unknown. *About David* by Susan Beth Pfeffer (Laurel Leaf, 1980), cover artist unknown. **PAGE 188:** *Breaking Camp* by Steven Kroll (Scholastic, 1985), cover artist unknown. **PAGE 190:** *Kessa* by Steven Levenkron (Warner Books, 1986), cover artist unknown. *Early Disorder* by Rebecca Josephs (Fawcett, 1980), cover artist unknown. **PAGE 191:** *Jay's Journal* by Anonymous (Beatrice Sparks) (Pocket, 1979), cover art by Mort Engel Studio. *Flowers in the Attic* by V. C. Andrews (Pocket Books, 1979), cover art by Gillian Hills. **PAGE 193:** *The Trouble with Wednesdays* by Laura Nathanson (Putnam, 1986), cover artist unknown. *Uncle Vampire* by Cynthia D. Grant (Atheneum, 1993), cover artist unknown. **PAGE 194:** *Now That Andi's Gone* by Karle Dickerson (Willowisp, 1994), cover artist unknown. *One Last Wish: A Season for Goodbye* by Lurlene McDaniel (Bantam, 1995), cover art by Christine Rodin. **PAGE 195:** *I Want to Live* by Lurlene McDaniel (Bantam, 1987), cover art by Jim Galante. **PAGE 198:** *It Happened to Nancy* by Anonymous (Beatrice Sparks) (Avon, 1994), cover artist unknown. **PAGE 199:** *What You Don't Know Can Kill You* by Fran Arrick (Laurel Leaf, 1992), cover artist unknown. **PAGE 201:** *What If They Knew?* by Patricia Hermes (Dell Yearling, 1980), cover artist unknown. **PAGE 203:** *Unwed Mother* by Gloria D. Miklowitz (Grosset & Dunlap, 1977), cover artist unknown. *The Girls of Huntington House* by Blossom Elfman (Bantam, 1972), cover artist unknown. **PAGE 204:** *No More Saturday Nights* by Norma Klein (Ballantine, 1988), cover artist unknown. *What Kind of Love?* by Sheila Cole (Avon, 1995), cover artist unknown. **PAGE 206:** *My Darling, My Hamburger* by Paul Zindel (Bantam, 1969), cover artist unknown. **PAGE 207:** *Promises Are for Keeping* by Ann Rinaldi (Bantam, 1982), cover art by Derek James. **PAGE 208:** *Unbirthday* by A. M. Stephensen (Avon, 1982), cover artist unknown. *Beginner's Love* by Norma Klein (Fawcett, 1983), cover artist unknown. **PAGE 212:** *Die Softly* by Christopher Pike (Archway, 1993), cover artist unknown. **PAGE 215:** *Family Crypt* by Joseph Trainor (Dell, 1984), cover artist unknown. *Slumber Party* by Christopher Pike (Scholastic, 1985), cover artist unknown. *Goosebumps #45: Ghost Camp* by R. L. Stine (Scholastic, 1996), cover artist unknown. **PAGE 217:** *Down a Dark Hall* by Lois Duncan (Laurel Leaf, 1974), cover artist unknown. *Stranger with My Face* by Lois Duncan (Little Brown & Co, 1981), cover artist unknown. **PAGE 218:** *The Dollhouse Murders* by Betty Ren Wright (Scholastic, 1983), cover artist unknown. **PAGE 219:** *The Secret Window* by Betty Ren Wright (Scholastic, 1982), cover artist unknown. **PAGE 220:** *Ghosts Beneath My Feet* by Betty Ren Wright (Scholastic, 1984), cover artist unknown. **PAGE 221:** *Behind the Attic Wall* by Sylvia Cassedy (Avon, 1983), cover artist unknown. *Wait Till Helen Comes* by Mary Dowling Hahn (Avon, 1986), cover artist unknown. **PAGE 222:** *Scared Stiff* by Jahnna N. Malcolm (Apple, 1991), cover artist un-

known. **PAGE 223:** *The Ghost of Graydon Place* by Dorothy Francis (Scholastic, 1982), cover artist unknown. **PAGE 224:** *The Secret Circle* by L. J. Smith (Harper, 1999), cover art by Daniel Weiss Associates Inc. **PAGE 225:** *The Baby-Sitter* by R. L. Stine (Scholastic, 1989), cover artist unknown. *Spring Break* by Barbara Steiner (Scholastic, 1996), cover artist unknown. **PAGE 226:** *Fear Street: The New Girl* by R. L. Stine (Archway, 1989), cover art by ENRIC. *Fear Street: The Knife* by R. L. Stine (Archway, 1992), cover artist unknown. **PAGE 227:** *Fear Street: The Prom Queen* by R. L. Stine (Archway, 1992), cover artist unknown. *Fear Street: The Thrill Club* by R. L. Stine (Archway, 1994), cover artist unknown. **PAGE 228:** The *Eternal Enemy* by Christopher Pike (Archway, 1993), cover artist unknown. The Midnight Club by Christopher Pike (Simon Pulse, 1994), cover artist unknown. **PAGE 230:** *Twisted* by R. L. Stine (Scholastic, 1987), cover artist unknown. *Nightmare Hall: Sorority Sister* by Diane Hoh (Scholastic, 1994), cover artist unknown. **PAGE 234:** *My Secret Admirer* by Carol Ellis (Scholastic, 1989), cover artist unknown. **PAGE 235:** *Silent Witness* by Carol Ellis (Scholastic, 1994), cover artist unknown. *The Mall* by Richie Tankersley Cusick (Archway, 1992), cover artist unknown. *My Secret Admirer* by Carol Ellis (Scholastic, 1989), cover artist unknown. **PAGE 236:** *The Boyfriend* by R. L. Stine (Scholastic, 1990), cover artist unknown. *The Girlfriend* by R. L. Stine (Scholastic, 1991), cover artist unknown. **PAGE 237:** *The Dead Girlfriend* by R. L. Stine (Scholastic, 1991), cover art by Broeck Steadman. **PAGE 239:** *The Ghosts of Departure Point* by Eve Bunting (Point, 1982), cover artist unknown. *Ghost Behind* Me by Eve Bunting (Archway, 1984), cover art by Michael Deas. **PAGE 240:** *The Last Vampire* by Christopher Pike (Archway, 1993), cover artist unknown. **PAGE 241:** *Vampire's Love #1: Blood Curse* by Janice Harrell (Scholastic, 1995), cover artist unknown. **PAGE 243:** *Sweet Valley High #104: Love and Death in London* by Francine Pascal (Bantam, 1994), cover art by Daniel Weiss Associates Inc. *Sweet Valley High #105: A Date with a Werewolf* by Francine Pascal (Bantam, 1994), cover art by Daniel Weiss Associates Inc.

Index

Acknowledgments

No book is easy to write—not even one about how rad Sweet Valley High was. And so I would like to thank the small, dedicated group of individuals who kept me from being kidnapped by a cult, lost at sea, or menaced by my secret evil third twin over the course of writing this book. Your efforts are deeply appreciated.

This book would not exist without genius literary agent Yfat Reiss Gendell, who offers me endless insight and support, despite the fact that she is way too cool to be hanging out with me. Thanks to everyone at Foundry, and special thanks to Jessica Felleman.

This book would also not exist without Blair Thornburgh at Quirk Books, the visionary who realized that my hideous compulsion to buy teen novels on eBay could be harnessed for good. Blair offered immeasurable encouragement, constantly came up with ways to improve this book, and indulged me every time I had a new "insight" into the Sleepover Friends. Who could ask for anything more in an editor?

Thanks to Andie Reid, Jane Morley, and Mary Ellen Wilson for making this a real, live book, and to Nicole De Jackmo, Ivy Weir, and Kelsey Hoffman, who are publicity and marketing masterminds. Thanks to Ricky Mujica for painting a gorgeous cover I'd like to hang in my bedroom (yes, I am 35).

Thanks to everyone who gave me insight into '80s and '90s middle grade and YA, whether through their professional expertise or their real-life experience: Rhys Bowen, Michael Cart, Caroline Cooney, Richie Tankersley Cusick, Wade Hudson and Cheryl Willis Hudson, Terry Hung, Mallory Kass, Lindsay Katai, Marie Myung-Ok Lee, Caren Lissner, Jessie Male, Dr. Cathryn Mercier, Constance Myers, Kelly Nugent, Nichole O'Connor, Christopher Pike, Kathryn Quealy, Candice Ransom, Emi Soekawa, Hodges Soileau, Broeck Steadman, and Deborah Stevenson.

Blogs like the singular *Cliquey Pizza*, Robin Hardwick's *The Dairi Burger*, and Kim Hutt's *What Claudia Wore*, as well as podcasts like Kelly Nugent and Lindsay Katai's *Teen Creeps*, work tirelessly to document this era in American literature (and examine why we grown-ups cannot stop obsessively going back to them). Check them out.

Thanks to my own personal Unicorn Club: Emma Lord, Erin Mayer, Simone Meltesen, Anna Parsons, Jennifer Williams, and Lady Sea Pickle Meltesen-Williams. Extra special thanks to Theresa Molter for being the first person to teach me that adults could love YA novels, even if they had questionable literary value.

Jesse Rifkin, I dumped Todd Wilkins to be with you and I'd do it again in a heartbeat.